MORE
MAKING BOOKS
BY HAND

QUARRY

MORE

MAKING BOOKS BY HAND

Exploring Miniature Books,
Alternative Structures, and Found Objects

Written and illustrated by
Peter and Donna Thomas

QUARRY BOOKS

First published in the United States of America by
Quarry Books, a member of
Quayside Publishing Group
100 Cummings Center
Suite 406-L
Beverly, Massachusetts 01915-6101
Telephone: (978) 282-9590
Fax: (978) 283-2742
www.quarrybooks.com

Library of Congress Cataloging-in-Publication Data
Thomas, Peter (Peter R.)
   More making books by hand: exploring miniature books, alternative structures, and found objects / Peter Thomas and Donna Thomas.
      p.   cm.
   ISBN 1-59253-074-5 (pbk.)
   1. Bookbinding—Handbooks, manuals, etc. 2. Book design—Handbooks, manuals, etc. 3. Miniature books. 4. Artists' books. I. Thomas, Donna (Donna Sue) II. Title
   z271.t47 2004
   686. 3—dc22   2004008830
                                                                      CIP

ISBN-13: 978-1-59253-074-8
ISBN-10: 1-59253-074-5

10 9 8 7 6 5

Design: Jean DeBenedictis
Cover Image: Allan Penn Photography
Illustrations: Donna Thomas
Copy Editor: Karen Levy
Proofreader: Stacey Ann Follin

Printed in Singapore

Paradise, 1999. 2¾" x 2" (7 cm x 5.1 cm). The text on the front of the flaps is intended to make the reader think of filing card dividers for thoughts about paradise. The text on the back of the flap is a quote by Dante. The panels are covered with handmade paper printed with images of a tropical paradise. The book is covered with handmade paper that has been printed with the word "paradise" in different colors and typefaces. 42 copies.

Contents

How to Cover the Bookblock   42

Section II: The Projects   54

The word "book," like the word "art," defies simple definition. Just as there are many kinds of art, there are many kinds of books: textbooks, comic books, pop-up books, fine press books, altered books, conceptual books. The list is limited only by imagination and creativity.

Artists' books are, by definition, works of art in the medium of the book. As it is with other kinds of art, books frequently beg questions of the viewer—What *is* art? What *is* a book? Not all books are works of art; some are simply storage units made to house information. A blank book is an empty container, but when you fill it, it becomes an artist's book that can share your ideas, feelings, imagery, and aesthetic with whoever views it.

Note: Unless otherwise noted, all featured books have been made by Peter and Donna Thomas.
Hand-rendered illustrations and linoleum block prints by Donna Thomas. Paper handmade by Peter Thomas.

Our book will introduce you to many tips and special techniques that we have developed for making many different kinds of books. It describes the tools we use and how we use them, and it describes common materials and ways you can use them to make books. We encourage you to strive for excellence in craftsmanship: if your craftsmanship is not as good as your idea, your book will be less likely to succeed as a work of art.

One day when we were selling blank books at a crafts fair, an old bookbinder came by and told us, "You can't buy experience." It was sound advice. The only way to become a book artist is to practice. Make a lot of books, hone your skills, and in time you will master the craft. This book will teach you how to build many book structures, but it will be up to you to fill those books with words and images, and to make them works of art.

Wildflowers of the John Muir Trail, 2003.
2⅝" x 2¼" (6.7 cm x 5.7 cm).

A single piece of paper is often called a *page*, *sheet*, or *leaf*. It has a front and a back. The front is called the *recto* and the back the *verso*. The *recto* is typically the odd-numbered page.

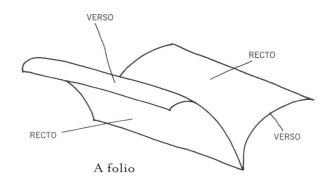

A folio

The rough, feathered edge of handmade paper is called the *deckle*. It is created when the deckle, which is also the name for the top half of the wooden frame that a papermaker uses to make paper, is removed. The pulp slumps and leaves a natural ragged edge. The fibers in paper tend to run in one direction, and this is called the *grain*. Paper folds more easily along the grain than across the grain. When commercial paper is cut and packaged, the label indicates grain direction, either by stating *grain long* (grain runs the length of the sheet) or *grain short* (the width) or by underscoring the dimension of the grain direction (for example, 8½" x <u>11</u>" paper has grain running in the 11" direction and is *grain long*).

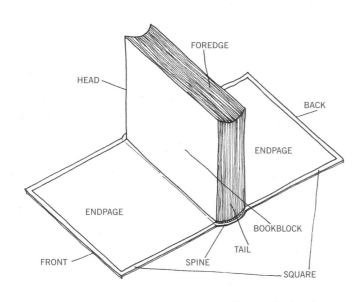

Parts of a book

When a sheet of paper is folded in half it is called a *folio*. A folio has four pages—two rectos and two versos. Folded pages that have been nested together are called a *section*. Sequential pages with some form of writing or illustration are called a *textblock*. The sections of a printed textblock are called *signatures*. This is because traditionally printers left small marks, or signatures, in the margins to indicate how the pages should be folded and their order in the text. When a textblock has *endpages* attached and is ready for binding, it is then called a *bookblock*.

There are terms for describing the parts of a book. The top is the *head* and the bottom is the *tail*. The pages turn at the *foredge* and are attached at the *spine*. The first and last pages of the bookblock are called *endpages*. *Front* and *back* are used to refer to both the covers of the book and the bookblock. The dimensions of a book are conventionally described by first stating the height and then the width.

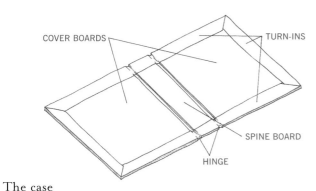

The case

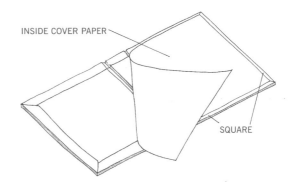

The square and inside cover paper

Most modern books are made by gluing a bookblock into a *case*. A typical case is made with *cover boards* and a *spine board* glued to a piece of *cover material*. There is a space on each side of the spine for a *hinge*. The cover material that wraps around the edges of the cover is called a *turn-in*. The edges of the cover that overhang the bookblock are called the *square* of the book. Some of our bindings have an *inside cover paper* that is glued inside the case before the bookblock is *cased-in*.

Note: For additional reference, a complete alphabetical glossary can also be found on page 140.

Tools

Traditional bookbinding required the use of many specialized tools, but it is not necessary to have those tools to make books; almost everything you need can be bought in art supply or hardware stores. We recommend the following tools for the beginning book artist: acrylic paintbrush, awl, binder clips, bone folder, butter knife, clamps, cutting mat, metal ruler, needle, pencil, sandpaper, scissors, thread, triangle, utility knife, and waxed paper.

Acrylic paintbrush. We use inexpensive brushes made for acrylic painting, and prefer stiff rather than soft synthetic bristle brushes. We use ½" to ¾" (1.3 cm to 1.9 cm) *flat* or *bright* brushes for small work. We use both flat and round 1" to 2" (2.5 cm to 5.1 cm) brushes for large work.

Awl. We use two awls—one with a short needle for marking and measuring, the other with a thicker needle for stabbing holes through cardboard or paper. You can make an awl by drilling a hole in a dowel, filling the hole with epoxy, and pushing a needle into the hole. An awl for bookbinding should have a straight shaft rather than a shaft that tapers. You can also use an electric drill to make holes in wood or very thick stacks of paper.

Binder clips (also sometimes called **bull clips**). We use these springing metal clips to hold paper during various bookbinding procedures. We keep several sizes—½" to 2" (1.3 cm to 5.1 cm)—on hand at all times.

Bone folder. We use a medium-sized folder with a point at one end and a curve on the other. Bone folders are usually made from cow bone and are available at art supply stores and from bookbinding suppliers. Some people use Teflon folders because they do not leave burnish marks on paper.

Butter knife. We use a serrated butter knife to slit paper to get a rough edge that resembles handmade paper's deckle edge. The larger the serrations on the knife, the rougher the cut.

Clamps. We use clamps to hold work firmly in place. Bar clamps are available from hardware stores. Although they are more expensive, we find the best bar clamps are *single-handed opening and closing*, because these can be operated with one hand while holding the work with the other. We have four mini bar clamps and four 18" (45.7 cm) bar clamps.

Cutting mat. We use a self-healing cutting mat as a working surface when cutting and scoring paper. These mats are available at art supply and fabric stores. We have found that the thicker mats and the ones made with more flexible materials hold up better.

Metal ruler. We use a 12" (30.5 cm) metal ruler that indicates ⅛" (3 mm), 1/16" (1.6 mm), and 1/32" (8 mm) increments as well as centimeters. Do not use a ruler with a cork pad on the bottom. It will give inaccurate measurements and lead to crooked cuts.

Needle. We use needles made specifically for bookbinding that can be bought from bookbinding suppliers. These needles have an eye that is the same size as the shaft. Fabric and craft stores carry needles that will work just fine. We use number three and number five milliner needles and number one sharp needles (the larger the number, the smaller the needle).

Pencil. We use a hard pencil with a sharp point when we want accurate measurements and a soft pencil when we want a mark that is easy to erase.

Sandpaper. We usually use garnet paper, which is available at hardware stores. We sometimes use emery boards in place of sandpaper. Wide-padded emery boards work the best.

Scissors. We use the best-quality stainless steel craft scissors we can get; cheap scissors usually do not work well.

Thread. We use many different types of thread for bookbinding. Waxed and unwaxed linen, silk, and cotton thread are all available from bookbinding suppliers. Button and craft thread can be purchased from a fabric store.

Triangle. A triangle is used to square paper or board and to mark both 45- and 90-degree angles.

Utility knife. We use utility knives with break-off blades. We use a smaller-sized knife when cutting paper and a larger-sized one when cutting boards. Change the blades often; having a sharp tool is essential for successful cutting.

Waxed paper. We often use waxed paper in place of a bone folder. We also use waxed paper when pressing our finished books, both around the book to protect the covers and in the fold of the end page to keep it from sticking to itself.

Two tools that are not essential but make the bookbinder's life easier are a press and a paper cutter.

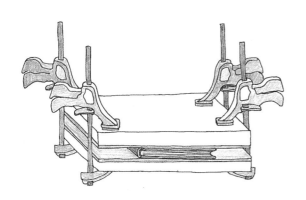 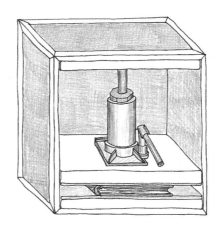

Press. (two shown above) A press is not essential when making miniature books, but for larger books it really does help to assure that glued surfaces will adhere and dry flat. The press commonly used by bookbinders is often called a *nipping press*. It is also known as a *copy press*, because before carbon paper it was used to make a blotter transfer copy from a handwritten document. If you cannot locate or afford to buy one of these presses, build one. A press can be made with four bar clamps and plywood faced with smooth, tempered hardboard (such as Masonite). Place the book between the boards, and use the clamps to apply pressure. A more complex press can be made using a metal or heavy plastic crate and a small car jack. The book is placed between boards, as in the first system, which are then placed in the bottom of the crate. The jack is set on top and is used to apply pressure. A piece of plywood may also need to be placed on top of the jack to reinforce the crate.

Paper cutter. A paper cutter is an invaluable tool for easily cutting paper and board square to the desired size. We have two kinds of paper cutters: a *guillotine paper cutter* and a *board shear*. The guillotine is used for cutting large stacks of paper into smaller sizes. The board shear is used for cutting single sheets of paper and cardboard. Both are big, heavy, and expensive pieces of equipment. Small versions of the board shear, called *lever cutters*, are available from art supply stores and bookbinding suppliers. These are great tools for a bookbinding studio. If possible, choose a lever cutter with a clamp. This will hold the paper or cardboard in place and keep it from twisting out of position while being cut.

The basic materials needed to make a book are paper, cardboard, covering materials (cloth, leather, and other materials), and adhesives.

PAPER

Beautiful handmade and art papers that are suitable for bookbinding can be bought from art supply and specialty paper stores. Commercial paper, both utilitarian and decorative, can be bought from office supply stores. Paper is said to be *archival* when it is not acidic and has an alkaline reserve. Archival paper should last hundreds of years before it turns brown or gets brittle. Cheaper papers (such as newsprint) may last only a few months or years before they begin to deteriorate. A pH-testing pen can be purchased from bookbinding supply stores and used to test whether a paper is acidic or not. Paper has grain, and in a book the grain should always run from head to tail. (See "How to Determine Grain Direction," page 16.)

We use our own handmade paper for most of the books we produce. Handmade paper can be very strong and usually has little noticeable grain. Strength is an important quality when the paper is used for a cover or as a hinge. Paper with a high rag, or cotton, content, although expensive, is usually much stronger than other commercial papers. Many beautiful art papers are not made from rag, so test their strength before use.

Commercial paper in the United States is made as a continuous sheet. It is cut and sold as *parent* sheets (for example, 23" x 35" for text or book paper, 17" x 22" for bond or office paper, and 26" x 40" for cover paper), and it is often sold in smaller sizes, packaged in 500-sheet *reams*. The *basis weight* of office paper ranges from 20 to 28 pound, text paper ranges from 60 to 80 pound, and cover paper ranges from 80 to 120 pound. A higher basis weight indicates greater thickness or density. However, 28-pound bond is about the same thickness as 70-pound text or 38-pound cover stock. This seeming discrepancy is explained by the fact that basis weight is calculated by using a ream of parent sheets, and those sizes are different for each type of paper. The commercial papers we use include bond, writing, text, index, and cover papers. We usually buy 70- to 80-pound book papers for our books.

In countries that use the metric system, commercial paper is sized using the A-format. This is a much simpler system. The series begins with A 0 which equals 1 square meter of paper, the dimensions of which are 841 mm x 1189 mm. When this sheet is folded or cut in half, the next smaller size is formed, A 1. The width of each size paper always equals the length of the next smaller size.

The standard sizes are as follows:

A 1 = 594 x 841 mm (one fold or cut out of A 0)
A 2 = 420 mm x 594 mm (two folds or cuts out of A 0)
A 3 = 297 mm x 420 mm (three folds or cuts out of A 0)
A 4 = 210 mm x 297 mm (standard letter and copy paper size)
A 5 = 148 mm x 210 mm (school notebooks)
A 6 = 105 mm x 148 mm (standard postcard size)

In the metric system, paper weight is always the weight of one square meter of paper, and is expressed in grams per square meter (gsm or g/m^2). The paper weight is easily calculated; for instance, the weight of 16 A 4 sheets will give you the weight of the paper in grams per square meter (because A 4 paper is four folds or cuts out of A 0). The standard writing or photocopy paper is 80 gsm. Postcard paper starts at 150 gsm and 500 gsm is a heavy cardboard.

CARDBOARD

There are many different kinds of cardboard products that can be used for binding. Binder's board is a special, very dense kind of board that is made of pressed paper pulp and sold by bookbinding suppliers. Binder's board is often called Davey board because the major manufacturer of the product in the USA was the Davey Company. Mat and museum boards are laminates made with several layers of paper and board glued together. Acid-free archival board and neutral-pH phase board, boxboard, or barrier board (all different terms for the same item) are available from conservation supply companies.

Cardboard, like paper, has grain, and in a book the grain should always run from head to tail. The thicker the board, the harder it is to cut but the less likely it is to warp when glued. Choose a board that is dense and strong and that does not curl after the glue dries. The thickness should be in proportion to the dimensions of the book and the weight of the paper. Heavyweight board measures between 0.09" (2.3 mm) and 0.075" (1.9 mm). Mediumweight board measures between 0.075" (1.9 mm) and 0.04" (1 mm). Lightweight board measures between 0.04" (1 mm) and 0.02" (0.5 mm). Two-ply mat board is usually ½₂" or 0.03" (0.75 mm) thick, and four-ply mat board is usually ⅛₆" or 0.06 (1.6 mm) thick.

CLOTH

There are special nonporous bookbinding cloths and paper-backed fabrics made specifically for bookbinding. These can be purchased from bookbinding suppliers. Regular fabric, which comes in many beautiful colors and textures, can also be used for bookbinding. Some fabrics work better than others. If a cloth has a loose weave, adhesives may seep through and leave a stain on the cover.

LEATHER

Leather is the archetypal material for covering books. Most binders prefer to use Nigerian goat leather (often called Moroccan leather) that is tanned specifically for bookbinding. Garment and craft leathers can also be used, but only trial and error can tell whether a particular leather will prove satisfactory for binding. Leather can be used just like cloth or paper, but most leather needs to be skived, or thinned down, at the turn-ins. This is done using a sharp knife and is a skill that takes much practice to master.

ADHESIVES

"Adhesive" is the general term for materials used to stick two different surfaces together. In this text, the word *glue* will be used as a general term for applying adhesive, even when it refers to a process using paste or other adhesives.

In the past, bookbinders made *hide glue* from animal skin and bone, and they made paste from wheat or rice flour. Today, adhesives are commonly available, and binders usually buy their glue. PVA (polyvinyl acetate), or white glue, has generally replaced hide glue, and glue stick or methyl cellulose is often used in place of paste. Other modern adhesives, including silicon, epoxy, cement, and adhesive tape, can be used for bookbinding, but they need to be used with caution because some of them are not archival. Rubber cement and cellophane tape should never be used; they will cause paper to deteriorate within only a few years of application.

Once the tools and materials for bookbinding have been acquired, you will need to know what to do with them. This section presents basic information about how to bind a book. These techniques will be used to make the books described in the projects that follow, but when understood, they will do more than just help you to follow instructions; these skills will enable you to create unique artists' books on your own.

HOW TO DETERMINE GRAIN DIRECTION

1. One test is to tear the piece of paper; paper always tears more easily with the grain. Another test is to roll the paper or drape it over the edge of a table; paper will bend more easily with the grain.

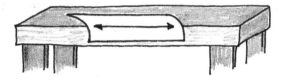

A final test is to get the paper wet; paper will curl with the grain.

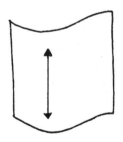

2. All the materials used to make a book should have their grain running from head to tail. When the grain runs head to tail, the pages will drape from the spine to the foredge. This will make the pages easy to turn and the book stay open. Paper and cardboard expand and contract with changes in humidity. When various glued layers are oriented with the grain in the same direction they will expand and contract in the same direction, and this will minimize warping in the finished book.

3. Always check the grain direction of precut paper (such as photocopy paper) before using it to make a book. For example, 8½" x 11" (21.6 cm x 27.9 cm) copy paper is usually cut grain long. If it is folded in half to make an 8½" x 5½" (21.6 cm x 14 cm) book, the grain will be running in the wrong direction.

Tip: If you want to use photocopies to make an 8½" x 5½" (21.6 cm x 14 cm) book, buy 11" x 17" (27.9 cm x 43.2 cm) paper, which usually comes grain long, and cut it in half.

HOW TO SQUARE MATERIAL BEFORE MEASURING

1. Before measuring, it is important to make sure the paper or cardboard is square.

2. Use a T square, L square, or triangle to check that all four corners are 90-degree angles.

3. If the material is not square, use these tools to mark and then cut it square.

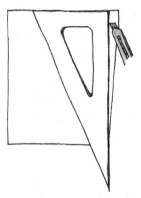

4. The lines of a cutting mat can also be used to square materials: Line up one edge of the material to be squared with a line on the mat, then use the vertical and horizontal lines and ruler marks on the mat as guides to square the other three edges.

HOW TO MARK ACCURATE MEASUREMENTS

The hole made by the point of an awl is smaller and therefore more accurate than a mark made with lead or ink.

1. When marking measurements with an awl, it is best to work on a receptive surface, such as a cutting mat.

2. If possible, make the mark in a fold where it will be hidden or in an outer margin that will later be cut off.

3. The hole poked by an awl can usually be made invisible by rubbing it shut with a fingernail or bone folder.

Tip: To line a ruler between two marks quickly and accurately, place the tip of the bone folder, pencil, or utility knife in the top hole. Slide the top end of the ruler up against it, then visually align the other end to the other mark. Press the ruler firmly to the surface and draw the tool along the edge to make the line, score, or cut.

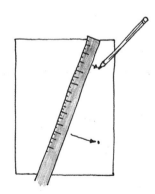

HOW TO MAKE A SCORED LINE TO FOLD PAPER

A fold can be creased in paper either by hand pressure or with a bone folder. To assure a straight fold, especially when folding across the grain, it is often necessary to score a line first, then fold.

1. It is best to score on a cutting mat, because the mat gives way to the pressure of the bone folder, accentuating the depression of the scored line.

2. Mark the location of the fold, and align a ruler between the two points.

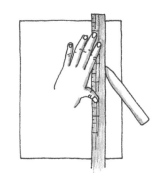

3. Draw along the edge of the ruler with the pointed end of a bone folder to create a shallow indented line, or score, in the paper. ●◆
If the point of the bone folder is too wide, use some other blunt tool (such as the back of a butter knife).

4. Fold and crease along the scored line.

HOW TO CUT PAPER AND CARDBOARD

We use a board shear in our studio, but when traveling we cut paper and board with a utility knife on a cutting mat. Before we owned the shear, if we had a lot of cutting to do, we would take our paper and board to a print shop or bindery and pay to have it cut to size.

1. To cut paper: Place the paper on a cutting mat. Measure and mark the cuts. Hold the ruler down firmly and draw the utility knife blade lightly along the ruler. The trick is to work on a cutting mat, have a very sharp blade, and apply light but firm and even pressure.

2. To cut thicker paper or cardboard: Follow the same steps described for cutting paper, but use the large utility knife. You may want to cut on a piece of scrap cardboard instead of a cutting mat; we have sliced into mats, ruining their surface, while cutting cardboard.

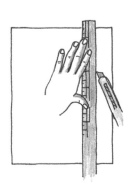

It is not necessary—or even recommended—to complete the cut in a single stroke. Make a number of passes, each following the exact path of the cut before. Too much pressure will cause the ruler to get pushed out of alignment or the blade to veer off in the wrong direction. The trick is to take your time when cutting cardboard. It is not easy, so relax and don't be in a hurry. ●◆

HOW TO OBTAIN A FEATHERED EDGE

1. Tear along a fold, rip against a beveled or deckle-edged ruler, or cut with scissors that have deckle-patterned blades.

2. To feather using a knife: Place a sheet of paper on a cutting mat. Mark, score if necessary, and crease the fold. Leave the paper folded in half. Use a serrated butter knife to saw through the valley fold. The cutting action should occur when pulling toward the fold. To get a rougher edge, either use a knife with larger serrations or saw several sheets at a time.

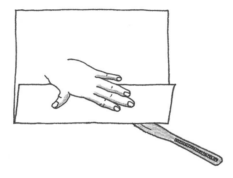

3. To feather using sandpaper: Mark the line you want to have feathered. Align it with a hard edge, such as a piece of metal, and then sand through the paper. Sand from the center, over the metal edge, toward the outside edge of the paper.

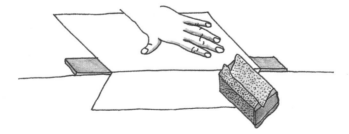

4. To feather using water: Score where the tear is desired. Dampen the score with water using a paintbrush. Wait a few moments for the fibers to soften, and then pull the paper apart along the score. (This will work with both straight lines and curves.)

HOW TO CHOOSE AND MODIFY ADHESIVES

There are five important qualities to consider when choosing an adhesive:

1. *Archival.* Will the adhesive remain stable and not damage the adhered surfaces?

2. *Tack.* How quickly and securely will the surfaces, turn-ins, and corners stick together?

3. *Spread.* How easy is it to cover the surface with the adhesive?

4. *Open time.* How long do you have to work before the adhesive dries? Will the glue dry before the boards are in place and the corners and turn-ins have been made?

5. *Reversible.* How easy is it to take apart two surfaces after they have dried together? It is generally easier to repair or conserve a book if the adhesive is reversible.

Paste can be made from ordinary flour. Paste, specifically designed for bookbinding, and methyl cellulose (a pastelike material made for the conservation binder) are both available from bookbinding suppliers. Paste and methyl cellulose are generally easy to spread and stay open a long time, but they are not very tacky until they begin to dry. Additionally, these adhesives are reversible and can usually be washed off without leaving a stain, which is not always true with PVA. Methyl cellulose is archival. Paste made from flour can mold, and dried paste in a book can attract book-damaging insects.

PVA is a generic name. The first company to sell it widely was the White Company, thus the name *white glue*. PVA is generally very tacky and stiff to spread, and has a much shorter open time than paste. It is generally not reversible and is generally archival. PVA sold at office supply, art supply, and fabric stores as craft glue is often hard to spread. It can be diluted with water to improve the spread, but thin and watery glue can cause papers to buckle and make them difficult to handle. One solution is to thin PVA with methyl cellulose or paste instead. This will increase the spread without making the glue watery. The qualities of PVA sold for bookbinding vary significantly, so if one brand does not perform as desired, try another.

Technical notes: To mix methyl cellulose with a PVA, add methyl cellulose, teaspoon by teaspoon, to the PVA until the PVA spreads easier. (The methyl cellulose should be the consistency of pea soup.) Sometimes a little water will also need to be added. When gluing metal, plastic, or found objects, use epoxy, cement (plastic or rubber), or silicon.

HOW TO APPLY GLUE

1. Always glue or paste on scrap paper. After applying the glue, discard the scrap paper or move your work. Glue stains can ruin an otherwise perfect book.

2. Always brush from the center toward the edge. Brushing over an edge toward the center may get adhesive on the wrong side of the material.

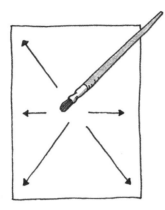

3. Work quickly. If the adhesive dries before the work is pressed together, the surfaces will not adhere.

4. Always press after gluing. Use a press or apply pressure by hand, with waxed paper or a bone folder, to make sure the surfaces have bonded and there are no wrinkles or hidden air bubbles.

5. Dry work under restraint. Use a press or weights to keep work from curling or warping as it dries. An hour may be enough drying time for a miniature book made with undiluted PVA, but larger surfaces and work that has been pasted will take longer to dry. It is always better to leave things to dry overnight.

6. To minimize curl when gluing: When adhesive is applied to paper, the fiber bonds relax and the paper expands. The more moisture in the adhesive and the more porous the paper, the more potential there is for expansion. When paper dries, it shrinks back to its original size and will curl toward the side that was glued. Theoretically, if glue is applied to both sides of a sheet of paper, it will dry flat.

If paper is glued to cardboard, the paper will stretch more than the cardboard. When dry, the cardboard will curl toward the paper. Because cardboard stretches less than paper, one way to minimize curl is to apply glue to the cardboard. Another way to minimize curl is to equalize the forces. Do this by gluing a piece of paper to the back of the cardboard to create a reverse curl. This will offset the curl caused by gluing paper to the front of the cardboard, and it will leave the cardboard flat when dry.

Technical note: If the paper glued to the front stretches more than the paper on the back, then the cardboard will curl to the front side. To equalize the forces, apply two layers to the back, or apply glue to the cardboard on the front and to the paper on the back.

7. Some gluing tips: Always test materials to find how they will react to the glue before using them in a project. A piece of scrap paper can be used as a mask to create a straight line of glue. Use this technique when gluing on an endpage or tipping in a sample or an illustration.

Multiple tip-ins can be glued at one time by lining them up so that they are all glued in one brush stroke.

A foam roller can be used instead of a brush, and is especially handy when covering a large surface area with adhesive.

HOW TO PRESS AND RUB WITH WAXED PAPER

1. The instructions "press and rub with waxed paper" will appear constantly in this book.

2. "Press" means to push hard on the material to secure it in place.

3. "Rub with waxed paper" means to grab a small piece of waxed paper and rub the material to remove any wrinkles or air bubbles and make sure the two surfaces adhere.

4. When materials of two different thicknesses are being glued together, rub on the thinner material.

5. Sometimes this will require flipping the work over. Always return the work to the original orientation before proceeding to the next step.

6. A bone folder can be used instead of waxed paper.

7. If a material shows marks or is burnished by rubbing, place a piece of scrap paper over the work to protect its surface while rubbing.

HOW TO WORK WITH CLOTH

There is fabric made especially for bookbinding (such as the plastic-coated buckram made for textbooks and the beautiful Japanese paper-backed silks and rayons). But cloth purchased from fabric stores can be successfully used to make books; we have probably used (or tried to use) every kind of cloth that is made. There are two common problems encountered using regular fabrics to make books.

1. Cloth often has so much sizing that the turn-ins are almost impossible to stick down. To solve this problem, wash the fabric to remove the sizing or choose another fabric.

2. Adhesive can seep through the weave and stain the book's cover. This problem can be addressed in one of three ways:

■ Use PVA that has not been watered down.

■ Apply the glue to the cardboard rather than the fabric.

■ Use paste or methyl cellulose. These adhesives usually will not stain, even if they do seep through the weave.

The terms "textblock" and "bookblock" are often used interchangeably, but there is a technical difference: A textblock is stacked pages, sewn or unsewn, whereas a bookblock describes the pages when they are ready to be bound.

HOW TO MAKE A TEXTBLOCK WITH ACCORDION FOLDS

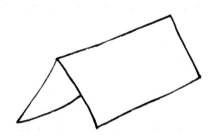

Mountain fold

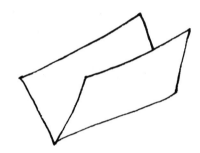

Valley fold

An accordion is made up of mountain and valley folds. Mountain folds are peaks that point toward you; valley folds are peaks that point away from you. We call each half of a mountain or valley fold a *page*. The accordion, as a book structure, has certain advantages over the sewn book: It can show more than two sequential pages at the same time, one page can flow into the next, and text can be generated on a copier or inkjet printer without the problems of registration and backup. Accordion books can also be displayed in a gallery or in a glass case with the entire text visible at once, so the content is easily grasped by the viewer.

How to Fold an Accordion

The goal in folding an accordion is to create a neat series of folds, with every page the exact same width, directly in line with the page before and after it. An accordion can easily be folded from a piece of paper that is four, eight, sixteen, or thirty-two times the desired width of each page without any extra measuring.

Note: These instructions can be used for any size book. Measurements are given in italics to make an accordion to fit the panel covers described in "How to Make Panel Covers and Attach an Accordion" (page 45).

1. Determine the page size. *2½" x 2" (6.4 cm x 5.1 cm)*

2. Multiply the page width by 8 (or 16 or 32). *16" (40.6 cm)*

3. Measure and cut the piece of paper for the accordion. Cut the paper so the grain runs in the same direction as the folds. *2½" x 16" (6.4 cm x 40.6 cm), grain short (the grain running in the 2½" [6.4 cm] direction)*

4. Fold the paper in half *2½" x 8" (6.4 cm x 20.3 cm) folio*

5. Open it again and lay it down flat, with the fold facing up (mountain fold).

6. Align the peak of the mountain fold with the left edge of the paper.

7. Press down on the right to crease the fold that is underneath the paper.

8. Bring the right edge of the paper so that it aligns with the left edge (and the peak of the mountain). Crease.

9. Open up the accordion. Reverse all valley folds so that there are only mountain folds.

10. Starting with the mountain fold closest to the left edge, bring each mountain to the left edge and crease.

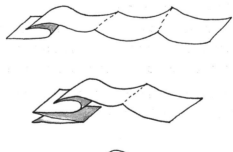

11. To complete the accordion, fold the right edge of the paper so that it aligns with the left edge (and the peaks of the mountain folds) and crease.

12. This will produce a perfect eight-page accordion with *eight 2½" x 2" (6.4 cm x 5.1 cm) pages.*

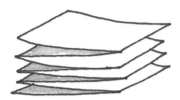

Technical note: The process can be repeated by making all folds mountain folds and following steps 9 and 10 as many times as required. *If repeated a second time, it will produce a 2½" x 1" (6.4 cm x 2.5 cm) 16-page accordion; if repeated a third time, 2½" x ½" (6.4 cm x 1.25 cm) 32-page accordion.*

How to Make Accordions from Single Sheets, Folios, and Other Accordions

1. Single sheets or accordions can be attached to one another using guards.

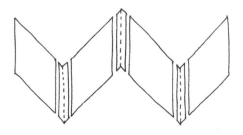

2. Folios or accordions can be glued or sewn at the foredge.

3. Single sheets, folios, or accordions can be made with hinges and attached by gluing or sewing.

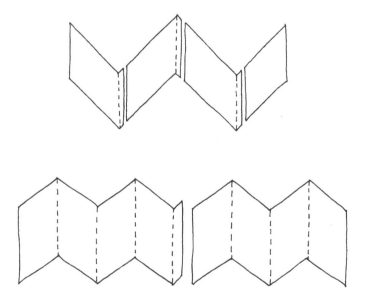

HOW TO MAKE A TEXTBLOCK WITH SEWN PAGES

When people think of bookbinding, they often think of sewing the pages together. Pages can either be stab sewn or sewn through folds.

1. *Sewing through folds.* The typical Western binding is made by sewing groups of folded pages together, usually sewing them to supporting cords or tapes. Other systems (for example, the long stitch, chain stitch, and unsupported sewing techniques such as the Coptic stitch) are also commonly employed.

2. *Stab sewing.* The traditional Asian binding has a textblock that is stab sewn. Single sheets of thin and flexible "rice" or mulberry paper are stab sewn along the spine with decorative stitching patterns. These papers are often translucent and the printing can show through the back, so many stab-sewn books are made using folios. These are sewn with the cut ends at the spine and the mountain fold at the foredge.

Each sewing system has advantages and disadvantages. Thick and stiff papers are best sewn through folds; they will not work well in a stab binding. Stab sewing can be used to make a book from paper printed on only one side, but it creates a book that will not lay open and is hard to read near the spine. Each method has different applications, and together they create the palette of sewing options for the book artist.

Tips for Sewing

1. Choose a needle that is the same size as the thread. The thread will be less apt to fall out of the first station, and it will be easier to control the thread's tension while sewing and tying the knots.

2. If you are having trouble threading a needle, try the other side of the eye. Because the eye of a needle is made by punching a hole through the shaft, it is easier to thread a needle in the direction in which the hole was punched.

3. Thread can be waxed by pulling it over a piece of beeswax. Waxed thread is less likely to fray or tangle and holds a knot tight.

4. If you want to secure the thread to the needle for sewing, just pass the point of the needle through the thread about 1" (2.5 cm) from the end. Pull on the needle until the thread is cinched up tightly against the needle.

5. If the thread breaks or is too short to finish sewing a section, attach a new length using a weaver's knot (see next page).

How to Tie a Weaver's Knot

1. Cut a new length of thread.

2. Cross the tail of the thread over itself to make a loop at one end.

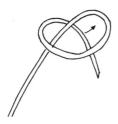

3. Loop the tail end of the thread partially through the first loop.

4. Pull on the thread to form the second loop.

5. Slip the broken end of the original thread through the second loop.

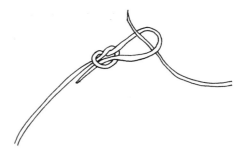

6. Pull both ends of the new thread to cinch down the loop over the original thread.

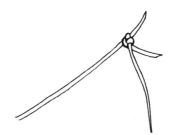

7. This will finish the weaver's knot and lock the new thread to the old thread end.

HOW TO MAKE A FOUR-HOLE STAB-SEWN TEXTBLOCK

To make the four-hole pattern commonly used in Asian bindings, begin with a stack of pages. Keep in mind that thin, flexible paper works better in stab-sewn books because it allows the book to open more easily.

Note: These instructions can be used for any size book. The measurements given are to make a textblock for Project 6: The Case-Bound Pocket Portfolio (see page 90). Using these measurements, the textblock will be 7" x 5" (17.8 cm x 12.7 cm).

1. Cut sheets of paper that measure 7" x 5" (17.8 cm x 12.7 cm) grain long (the 7" [17.8 cm] direction), and stack them together into a textblock.
Technical note: Alternatively, fold and stack folios, with the cut ends placed at the spine.

2. With a pencil, mark the four sewing stations on the top sheet of the textblock. The hole closest to the head will be called station A.

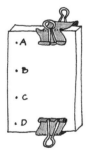

3. Mark all stations ⅜" (1 cm) away from the spine.

4. Mark station A ⅜" (0.95 cm) from the head.

5. Mark station D ⅜" (1 cm) from the tail.

6. Mark stations B and C equally spaced between stations A and D. The stations must be parallel to the spine, but the distance between the stations can vary.

7. Clamp the pages together using binder clips at the head and tail of the block.

8. Predrill the sewing stations with a very small drill bit, or poke holes with an awl. Make sure the needle and thread will fit through the hole.

9. Cut the thread.
Technical note: The thread will need to be about four to five times the length of the book. The length will vary based on the distance between the sewing stations and the spine and whether there are decorative sewing patterns.

10. Arrange the textblock so the spine faces you and station A is on the left.

11.
Begin sewing at station C.

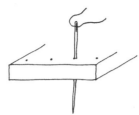

Stitch down through the spine of the book so that your needle comes out of C on the back of the book.

Pull the thread through so about 2" (5 cm) remains on the top of the textblock.

If the thread slips out of the hole, hold it in place with one of the binder clips.

12.
Circle the thread around the spine, then stitch again down through C so the thread encircles the spine and the needle ends up on the back.

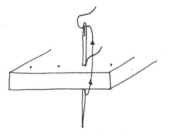

13.
Stitch up through the back of the book at B, circle the thread around the spine, and then stitch up through B again.

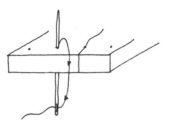

14.
Bring the thread directly over to station A, stitch down through the front of the book at A, circle the thread around the spine, and then stitch down through A again.

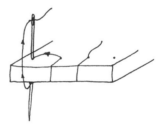

15.
Circle the thread around the head of the book (rather than the spine), and once again stitch down through A.

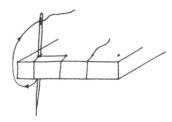

16. Run the thread along the back of the book, parallel to the spine, from station A to station B, and then stitch up through B.

17. Run the thread along the front of the book, parallel to the spine, from station B to station C, and then stitch down through C.

18. Run the thread along the back of the book, parallel to the spine, from station C to station D, and then stitch up through D.

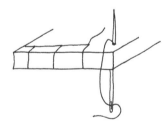

19. Circle the thread around the spine, then stitch up through D a second time so the thread encircles the spine and the needle ends up on the front side of the book.

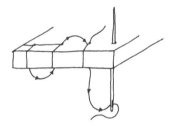

20. Circle the thread around the tail of the book (rather than the spine), and once again stitch up through D.

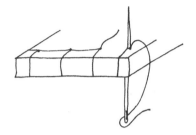

21. To finish off the sewing, run the thread along the front of the book, parallel to the spine, from station D to station C, and tie a double knot over the hole.

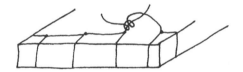

22. Cut the thread so that the ends are about ¼" (0.6 cm) long.

Technical notes: With larger books, the spacing from the head and tail will change.

There can be more stations, their locations can vary, and there are many variations to the basic stitch. Good examples can be found in *Japanese Bookbinding* by Kojiro Ikegami (New York: Weatherhill, 1986).

HOW TO SEW A SINGLE-SECTION TEXTBLOCK

A section is made by nesting folios. The stitch used to sew together a single section is called the pamphlet stitch. Single sheets can be guarded together as described in "How to Make Accordions from Single Sheets, Folios, and Other Accordions" (page 26) to create folios that can also be sewn using the pamphlet stitch. Traditionally, bookbinders began sewing the pamphlet stitch from the valley fold, so the final knot was inside the section.

Note: These instructions can be used for any size book. Measurements given use half of a legal size piece of paper (8½" x 14") to sew a single section that will be 7" x 4¼" (17.8 cm x 10.8 cm). The finished textblock may be inserted in the portfolio case described in Project 6.

STEP 1: PREPARE THE PAPER FOR SEWING

1. Cut five pieces of paper that measure 7" x 8 ½" (17.8 cm x 21.6 cm), grain short.

2. Fold the paper in half to make five 7" x 4¼" (17.8 cm x 10.8 cm) folios. It is most accurate to fold one sheet of paper at a time. Crease the fold with a bone folder or the heel of your hand.

3. Nest the folios together to make one section.

Use binder clips to hold the section together while sewing.

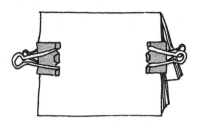

4. Use a pencil to mark three sewing stations on the spine of the section.

Mark the outer stations ⅜" (1 cm) from the head and tail.

Mark the third station halfway between the other two stations.

Technical note: The outer stations for the pamphlet stitch may be placed ¼" (0.6 cm) to ½" (1.3 cm) from the head and tail, depending on the page size.

5. Pre-poke the sewing stations using a needle or awl.

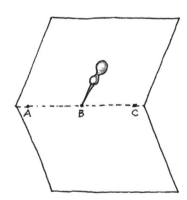

STEP 2: SEW THE SECTION TOGETHER

1. Cut a length of thread that is at least three times the height of the pamphlet, and thread the needle.

2. Designate the sewing station at the head as station A and place it on the left.

3. Stitch from the valley side, up through B, and pull the thread through, but leave 2" (5.1 cm) of thread inside the section.

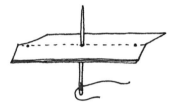

4. Stitch from the mountain down through A.

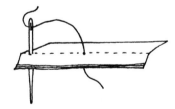

5. Run the thread along the valley fold, past B, and stitch up through C.

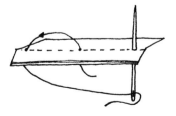

6. Stitch from the mountain down through B.

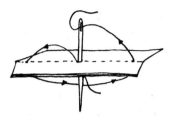

7. Make sure the two ends of the thread are on different sides of the thread that runs from C to A.

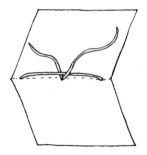

8. Tie the ends of the thread in a knot, as when tying a shoe, then repeat to make a double knot that will not pull loose.

9. Clip off the thread ends about ¼" (0.6 cm) from the knot. After tying the knot, tease the ends so they are fluffy instead of blunt.

Technical notes: A tall pamphlet may require more sewing stations, but there must always be an odd number of sewing stations.

When all pages of a section are the same size, the foredges will not be flush but will taper. To obtain a straight foredge, the section must either be trimmed after sewing or composed of pages that are, from the center out, each slightly larger than the next.

HOW TO SEW MULTIPLE SECTIONS FOR A MINIATURE TEXTBLOCK

When there are too many pages to sew in a single section, multiple sections are created and then sewn together. Miniature books and books with thick paper may have only one or two folios per section, but books with thin paper may have as many as 16 folios in a section. The system we use to sew miniature books employs two sewing stations.

Note: These instructions can be used for any miniature book. Measurements are given to make the four-section textblock for Project 2: The Miniature Case-Bound Book (see page 56). The textblock will measure 2¾" x 1¾" (7 cm x 4.4 cm).

STEP 1: PREPARE PAPER FOR SEWING

1. Cut eight pieces of paper for the textblock, each measuring 2¾" x 3½" (7 cm x 8.9 cm), grain short.

2. Fold the paper in half to make eight 2¾" x 1¾" (7 cm x 4.4 cm) folios.

3. Make four two-page sections.

4. Stack the folded sections on top each other. If there is text, arrange the sections with the heads to the left and the last section on the bottom.

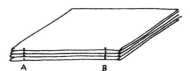

5. Use a pencil to mark each section with two sewing stations. Place the marks on the peak of the mountain fold, approximately ⅜" (1 cm) from both the head and the tail.

6. Make a second mark, in a different color, along the head of the book so it will be obvious if a section becomes reversed while sewing.

7. Open the sections and pre-poke the sewing stations with a needle or a small awl.

STEP 2: SEW THE SECTIONS TOGETHER

1. Cut a length of thread that is at least five times the height of a section, and thread the needle.

2. Designate the hole on the left in section 1 as "1A" ("1" refers to section 1, "A" to sewing station A). The same hole in section 2 will be 2A, and so on.

3. Begin sewing with section 4. (It is traditional to begin with the last section of the textblock.)

4. Stitch through the mountain at 4A, then out of the valley at 4B. Leave a 2" (5 cm) tail of thread at 4A.

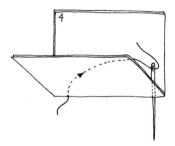

5. Place section 3 on top of section 4. Check the marks at the head to make sure the section is oriented correctly.

6. Stitch through the mountain at 3B, then out of the valley at 3A.

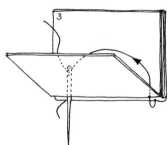

Pull on the thread to remove any slack. Pull gently to avoid breaking the thread, and to prevent the sections from curling into a convex curve at the spine. Pull in the direction of the sewing to avoid ripping the paper.

7. Tie the ends of the thread in a double knot.

8. Place section 2 on top of section 3.

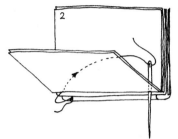

9. Stitch through the mountain at 2A, then out of the valley at 2B.

10. Pull on the thread to remove any slack.

11. Make a kettle stitch. To make a kettle switch, pass the needle and thread between sections 4 and 3 where the thread passes from 4B to 3B.

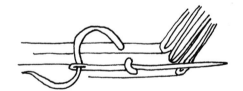

Pass the needle through the loop.

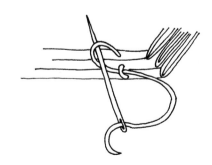

Pull gently on the thread to tighten the knot.

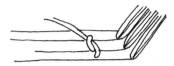

Tip: Pinch the sections together while tying the kettle stitch to keep the thread tight.

12. Place section 1 on top of section 2.

13. Stitch through the mountain at 1B, then out of the valley at 1A.

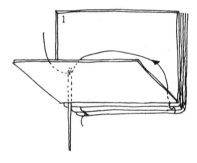

14. Tie a kettle stitch around the thread passing from 3A to 2A.

15. To finish the sewing, make a second kettle stitch as a double knot.

16. Trim the thread ends so they do not extend past the head or tail of the textblock.

Technical note: If there were more than four sections, the sewing would continue using the same sequence of steps.

HOW TO SEW MULTIPLE SECTIONS FOR A LARGE TEXTBLOCK

Larger books need to be attached at more than two sewing stations. The traditional technique employs a sewing frame, and wrapping the thread around a cord or tape at each sewing station connects the sections. We learned how to sew books on a frame by reading instructions in Pauline Johnson's *Creative Bookbinding* (New York: Dover, 1990). In 1974, we began traveling to sell blank books at craft fairs, and because of limited space we needed to find a way to sew multiple sections without a frame. Through trial and error we developed the following system.

Note: These instructions can be used to sew any size or shape textblock. Measurements are given to sew a horizontal format 4" x 5¼" (10.2 cm x 13.3 cm) textblock. This size textblock can be bound using the three-part case described in Project 5: The Accordion Pleat Spine Stab-Sewn Book (see page 82).

STEP 1: PREPARE PAPER FOR SEWING

1. Cut 20 pieces of paper that measure 4" x 10½" (10.2 cm x 26.7 cm), grain short.

2. Fold the paper into 4" x 5¼" (10.2 cm x 13.3 cm) folios, and make four five-page sections.

3. Stack the folded sections on top of each other. If there is text, arrange the sections with the heads to the left and the last section on the bottom.

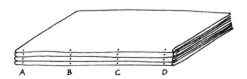

4. Use a pencil to mark each section with four sewing stations. Mark on the peak of the mountain fold.

5. Make marks that are ⅜" (1 cm) from the head and ⅜" (1 cm) from the tail.

6. Place the other two marks equally spaced between the marks at the head and tail. These will be about 1" (2.5 cm) from the other stations.

7. Make a second mark, in a different color, along the head of the book so it will be obvious if a section becomes reversed while sewing.

8. Pre-poke the sewing stations with a needle or small awl.

STEP 2: SEW THE SECTIONS TOGETHER

1. Cut a length of thread at least five times the height of a section, and thread the needle.

2. Designate the hole on the left in section 1 as "1A" ("1" refers to section 1, "A" to sewing station A). The same hole in section 2 will be 2A, and so on.

3. Begin with section 4. Stitch into the mountain at 4A, then out of the valley at 4B, then into the mountain at 4C, and then out of the valley at 4D. Leave a 2" (5 cm) tail of thread at 4A.

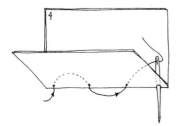

4. Place section 3 on top of section 4. Stitch through the mountain at 3D, then out of the valley at 3C.

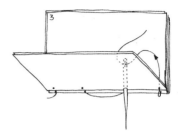

Stitch back into 4C a second time. (This connects the sections together at the station.)
Make sure not to sew through the thread that is already in the station.

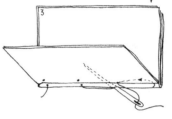

Stitch out of the valley at 4B a second time.

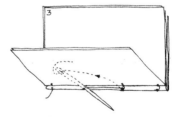

Stitch into the mountain at 3B. (This connects the sections.)

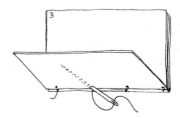

Stitch out of the valley at 3A.

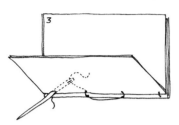

5. Pull on the thread to remove any slack inside the sections. Pull gently to avoid breaking the thread, ripping the paper, or pulling the sections into a convex curve at the spine.

6. Tie the ends of the thread in a double knot.

7. Place section 2 on top of section 3. Stitch into the mountain at 2A,

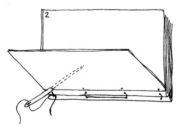

then out of the valley at 2B.

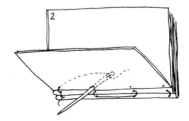

Stitch into the mountain at 3B a second time,

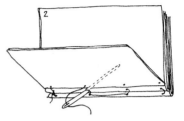

then out of the valley at 3C a second time.

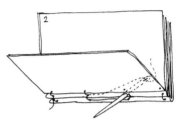

Stitch into the mountain at 2C,

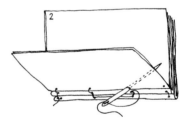

then out of the valley at 2D.

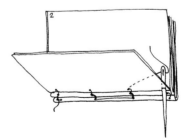

8. Pull on the thread to remove any slack.

9. Tie a kettle stitch where the thread passes from 4D to 3D. (See "How to Sew Multiple Sections for a Miniature Textblock," step 2, page 34.)

10. Place section 1 on top of section 2. Stitch into the mountain at 1D, then out of the valley at 1C.

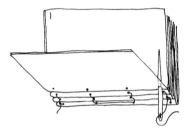

Stitch back into the mountain at 2C a second time, then out the valley at 2B a second time. Stitch into the mountain at 1B, then out of the valley at 1A.

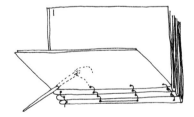

11. Pull on the thread to remove any slack.

12. Tie a kettle stitch where the thread passes from 3A to 2A.

13. To finish the sewing, make a second kettle stitch as a double knot.

14. Trim the thread ends so they do not extend past the head or tail of the textblock.

Technical notes: If there were more than four sections, the sewing would continue using the same sequence of steps. For tall books, it may be necessary to add more sewing stations.

HOW TO PREPARE THE TEXTBLOCK FOR BINDING

After a textblock is sewn, there are still several things that need to be done before it is ready to be bound. Once these preparations are complete, the textblock is then referred to as a bookblock.

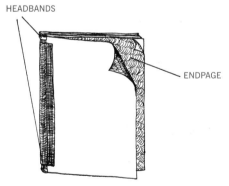

HEADBANDS

ENDPAGE

STEP 1: GLUE THE SPINE

If the spine of a multisection book is not glued together, gaps will show between the sections and the spine will sag and shift from a rectangle into a trapezoid.

1. Hold the textblock near the spine, applying light pressure.

2. Apply a thin coat of glue to the entire spine.

Do not apply glue with too much force; if glue is forced up between the sections they will not open completely.

3. After the glue dries, there is usually a slight swelling of the spine.

4. To remove the swelling, pound lightly with a hammer until the spine is the same thickness as the foredge. The spine can be slightly rounded at this time by pounding at an angle.

STEP 2: ATTACH THE ENDPAGES

A textblock can be bound (or cased-in) by gluing the outsides of the first and last pages to the insides of the covers. This method has a problem: Those pages are part of a folio. If the book receives heavy use and tears at the hinge, the other half of the folio will no longer be attached and can fall out.

To avoid this problem, attach the endpages to the outside of the textblock and glue them to the covers. Endpages may be thicker and stronger than the text paper, and they also may be marbled or decorated.

1. Cut two pieces of paper that, when folded, are the same size as the textblock. The grain should run along the fold.

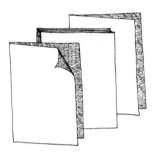

2. Place a piece of scrap paper as a mask on the bookblock, ½" (1.3 cm) from the spine.

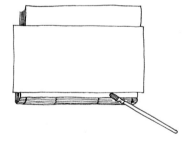

3. Apply glue, brushing toward the spine.

4. Remove and discard the scrap paper.

5. Align the endpage with the edges of the textblock.

6. Press at the spine and rub with waxed paper to ensure the endpage adheres.

7. Repeat the process with the other endpage.

STEP 3: APPLY THE SPINE LINING

Bookbinders often glue thin, loose-weave cotton or linen cloth, called *super* or *mull*, over the spine and endpages to reinforce the hinge.

1. Cut a strip of super that is slightly shorter than the textblock and wide enough to cover at least ½" (1.3 cm) of the endpage on both sides of the spine.

2. Apply a thin coat of glue to the spine and endpages.

3. Press the super over the glued area, and rub it with waxed paper to make sure it adheres.

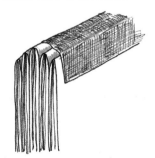

STEP 4: ATTACH THE HEADBANDS

Many books have headbands at the head and tail. Historically, these colorful bands of twisted thread were functional; they were sewn through the sections to provide support so that when books were pulled from the shelf the spine would not be ripped off. Today, most headbands are ornamental. Strips of headband material can be purchased from bookbinding suppliers or made by wrapping material around string. These are cut to size and glued to the spine. The use of ornamental headbands is a matter of taste. At a binding conference, we overheard a well-known binder commenting, "How tacky; I would never use a stick-on headband." But on the other hand, a bookbinder, looking at a book we made without headbands, commented, "A book is naked without a headband."

1. Cut two pieces of headband material, each the same width as the spine.

2. Apply glue to the spine at the head.

3. Press the headbands to the spine, with the colored bead facing the foredge and resting on top of the textblock.

4. Repeat steps 2 and 3 to attach the headband at the tail. For instructions on how to sew headbands, see Jane Greenfield's *Headbands: How to Work Them*. New Castle, Delaware: Oak Knoll Books, 1990.

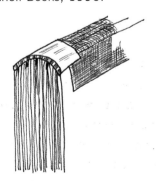

Books have either soft or hard bindings. Paperback books, folded paper covers and stab-sewn bindings are examples of soft bindings. Hardback book and Coptic bindings are examples of hard bindings. Most of the projects in this book have hard covers. The following techniques explain how to make hard covers for both accordion and sewn books.

HOW TO MAKE A CORNER

The library corner and the mitered corner are the two basic corners that bookbinders make. The library corner is found on most old textbooks. It is bulky, sturdy, and usually required when using fabric. (The library corner does not leave any cut edges exposed, and with cloth, cut edges can fray.) The mitered corner is the corner we most frequently use. It is a compact corner and is used with paper, book cloth, and leather. These instructions show how to make just one corner, but the steps can be practiced on each corner of your board.

How to Make a Library Corner
(Use with cloth, paper, book cloth, or leather.)

1. Glue a piece of cardboard to a larger piece of cloth.

2. Press and rub with waxed paper.

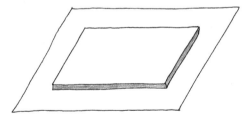

3. Trim the cloth so that the turn-ins are about ½" (1.3 cm) wide.

4. Apply a thin layer of glue to the cardboard at one corner.

5. Fold and press the material over the corner, creating a triangle with the two sides at 90-degree angles to the edge of the cardboard.

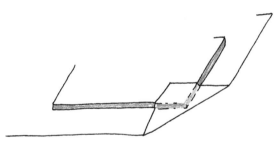

6. Apply glue to both the edge and the inside of the cardboard. (The glued area needs to be only as wide as the turn-ins.)

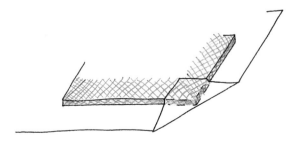

7. Fold the turn-ins over the cardboard, first one side, then the other.

8. The turn-ins will not meet exactly at the corner, but bring them as close together as possible.

9. Press and rub with waxed paper. Make sure the turn-ins adhere to both the edge and the inside face of the cover board.

How to Make a Mitered Corner

(Use with paper, book cloth, or thin leather.)

1. Glue a piece of cardboard to the undecorated side of a larger piece of paper.

2. Press and rub with waxed paper.

3. Trim the paper so that the turn-ins are about ½" (1.3 cm) wide.

4. Draw a line at a 45-degree angle to the edges of the cardboard. The line should be twice the thickness of the cardboard and away from the corner.

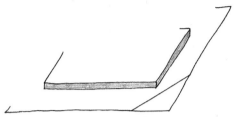

If the line is not at a 45-degree angle to the edges of the cardboard, the corner folds will end up crooked.

If the line is too close to the corner of the board, the cover material will not completely cover the cardboard.

If the line is too far away, the folds will not join perfectly at the corner.

With thicker cover paper, the space may need to be increased to three times the thickness.

Tip: A quick way to estimate where to make the line is to fold the cover paper over the corner of board, press it against the corner, and lightly crease the fold. Use the fold as a visual guide.

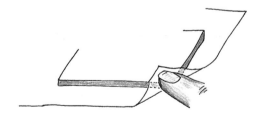

5. Cut off the corner, using the line as a guide.

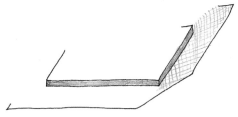

6. Apply glue to the turn-in that is to the right of the corner.

7. Fold the turn-in over the board. Make sure the turn-in adheres to both the edge and the inside of the cover board.

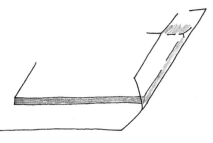

8. Press and rub with waxed paper.

9. Use a bone folder (or your thumbnail) to press a small triangular section at the corner of turn-in to the edge of the cardboard (left of the corner) and to the left of the turn-in.

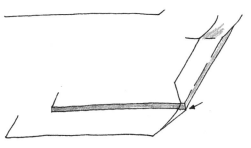

10. Apply glue to the turn-in on the left side of the corner.

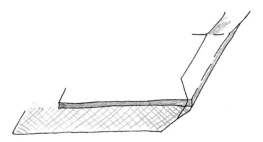

11. Fold the turn-in over the cardboard. If the corner is perfect, the folds will align at a 45-degree angle from the corner.

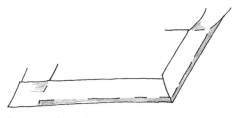

12. Press and rub with waxed paper.

HOW TO MAKE PANEL COVERS AND ATTACH AN ACCORDION

When an accordion is bound, the first and last folds are usually valley folds. The folds can function like the endpages of a sewn book, and panel covers can be attached to the endpages.

Note: These instructions can be used for any size book. Measurements are given (in italics) to make panel covers for the eight-page 2½" x 2" (6.4 cm x 5.1 cm) accordion bookblock described in "How to Fold an Accordion" on page 24. These are also the correct size to use as the panel covers for Project 2: The Accordion Book with Pockets (see page 62).

STEP 1: DETERMINE THE DIMENSIONS OF THE COVER BOARDS

1. The boards can simply be cut slightly longer and wider than the bookblock. *2⅝" x 2⅛" (6.7 cm x 5.4 cm) with 1/16" (1.6 mm) squares.*

Technical notes: To calculate the exact dimensions for the cover boards, first decide the width of the square, then double that and add it to the height and width.

The square should be equal on all four sides and in proportion to the size of the book.

The average square is between 1/16" (1.6 mm) and 3/16" (4.7 mm) wide.

A large book with thick boards will require a wider square than a miniature book with thin boards.

STEP 2: DETERMINE THE DIMENSIONS OF THE COVER MATERIAL

1. The cover material can simply be cut larger than the cover board. *3⅝" x 3⅛" (9.2 cm x 7.9 cm) with ½" (1.3 cm) turn-ins.*

Technical notes: To calculate the exact dimensions for the cover material, first decide the width of the turn-ins. Add the width of the turn-ins plus the thickness of the board to the height and width measurements of the boards.

The turn-ins must be long enough to wrap around the cover board and wider than the square of the book (so that they will be covered by the endpage).

To calculate this measurement, add the thickness of the cover board, the width of the square, and about ¼" (0.6 cm) to extend under the endpage.

STEP 3: PREPARE THE MATERIALS

1. Cut two pieces of cardboard for the cover boards, each measuring 2⅝" x 2⅛" (6.7 cm x 5.4 cm), grain long.

2. Cut two pieces of cloth to cover the panels, each measuring 3⅝" x 3⅛" (9.2 cm x 7.9 cm), grain long. (The cover can be made from other materials, such as paper, and the same instructions will apply.)

STEP 4: MAKE THE PANEL COVER

1. Place one piece of cloth face down on the work surface.

2. Apply glue to one cover board. Be sure to always apply glue on scrap paper and discard the scrap paper before proceeding.

3. Place the cover board in the center of the cloth. ●◆

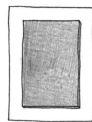

4. Press and rub with waxed paper.

5. If necessary, trim the edges of the cloth to create straight and equal turn-ins.

6. Decide which kind of corner you will use. If making a mitered corner, trim the corners. (See "How to Make a Mitered Corner," page 43.)

7. If making a library corner, stick down the corners. (See "How to Make a Library Corner," page 42.) Note: The illustrations here show library corners.

8. Apply glue to the cardboard at all four corners. Fold the cloth over the corners so that the cut edges of the corners are perfectly parallel to the board. Press in place. ●◆

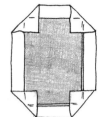

9. Apply glue to the cardboard and cloth corners, at both the head and the tail of the panel. ●◆
Make the corners and fold the turn-ins over the boards. Press and rub with waxed paper.

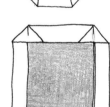

10. Repeat the process for the corners and turn-ins at the foredges. ●◆

11. Place the cover between sheets of waxed paper and under weights or in a press until dry.

12. Repeat the process to make a second panel.

STEP 5: APPLY A FILLER TO THE COVER PANEL

1. If the cover material is thin, a filler is not needed. If the cover material is very thick, the turn-ins may create a depression on the inside of the panel cover. This will need to be filled with thin cardboard to make the inside of the cover level. ●◆

2. Cut a piece of thin cardboard that is the same thickness as the cover material and slightly larger than the depression. *About 2⅛" x 1⅝" (5.4 cm x 4.1 cm), grain long.*

3. Center the cardboard filler over the turn-ins. ●◆

4. Draw a sharp utility knife around the filler, cutting through the turn-ins. ●◆

5. Remove the turn-ins from the area to be filled.

6. Apply glue to the filler, and press it into the inside of the cover. ●◆

STEP 6: GLUE THE ACCORDION TO THE PANEL COVERS

1. Designate the front and back covers, and make small marks with an awl inside both covers to indicate the squares and thus where to place the accordion. The marks will be ⅟₁₆" (1.6 mm) from each corner of the panel covers. ●◆

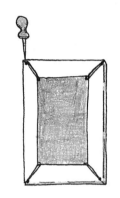

2. Place a sheet of scrap paper in the valley fold between the first and second pages of the accordion. If there is text or illustration, make sure it is oriented correctly. ●◆

3. Apply glue to the outside of the front endpage. Carefully remove and discard the scrap paper.

4. Align the page to the marks on the cover. Press it in place and rub with waxed paper.

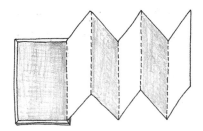

5. Repeat the process to attach the outside of the back endpage to the back cover.

Tip: When you gain some confidence, you'll be able to position the endpages by eye.

STEP 7: PRESS THE BOOK

1. Place waxed paper in the valley folds at each end of the accordion and around the covers.

2. Place the completed book under weight to dry. If the accordion bookblock has uneven folds or bulky pages, press only the covers.

HOW TO MAKE A CASE AND CASE-IN A BOOKBLOCK

Case binding is the term bookbinders use to describe the process of attaching a bookblock to a pre-made cover. This cover, or case, is made by wrapping three pieces of cardboard (two cover boards and a spine) with cloth, leather, or paper. The bookblock is cased-in to the case. Most books we make are case bound, and many of the structures we have developed are simple variations of the basic case binding.

Note: These instructions can be used for any size book. Measurements are given (in italics) to make the case binding for Project 1: The Miniature Case-Bound Book (see page 56). This case fits a miniature sewn bookblock that measures 2¾" by 1¾" (7 cm x 4.4 cm) and is ¼" (0.6 cm) thick.

STEP 1: DETERMINE THE DIMENSIONS OF THE COVER BOARDS

1. The cover boards can simply be cut slightly higher and slightly narrower than the bookblock. *2⅞" x 1¹¹⁄₁₆" (7.3 cm x 4.3 cm) with ¹⁄₁₆" (1.6 mm) squares.*

Technical note: Estimated dimensions for the cover boards and hinge won't always produce a book that opens easily and has even squares and a tight-fitting spine. Information is given in the technical notes at the end of this section describing how to calculate the exact dimensions by taking into consideration the width of the square, the thickness of the cardboard, and the width of the hinge.

STEP 2: DETERMINE THE DIMENSIONS OF THE SPINE BOARD

1. The spine board is the same height as the cover boards; the width is the thickness of the bookblock, plus the thickness of the two cover boards. 2⅞" x ⅜" (7.3 cm x 1 cm) Technical note: Binders often use a thinner, more flexible cardboard for the spine board.

Tip: A simple way to determine the width of the spine is to stack the two cover boards on top of the bookblock, apply light pressure, and measure the thickness with a ruler.

STEP 3: DETERMINE THE DIMENSIONS OF THE COVER MATERIAL

1. The dimensions of the cover material can generally be estimated by adding about 1" (2.5 cm) to the height of the cover boards and about 1½" to 2" (3.8 cm to 5.1 cm) to the width of the two cover boards and the spine board. 4" x 5¼" (10.2 cm x 13.3 cm) with ½" (1.3 cm) turn-ins and 3⁄16" (4.8 mm) hinges

STEP 4: PREPARE THE MATERIALS

1. Cut cover boards that each measure 2⅞" x 1¹¹⁄16" (7.3 cm x 4.3 cm), grain long.

2. Cut one spine board that measures 2⅞" x ⅜" (7.3 cm x 1 cm), grain long.

3. Cut one piece of medium-weight paper for the cover that measures 4" x 5¼" (10.2 cm x 13.3 cm), grain short.
Tip: To speed up cutting the cover boards and the spine, cut a long piece of cardboard to the required height. First cut the two cover boards, and then the spine board, from the same piece.

STEP 5: MAKE THE CASE

1. Place the cover paper facedown.

2. Apply glue to the spine board. Be sure to work on scrap paper, then discard the scrap paper before proceeding.

3. Place the spine board, centered, on the cover paper.

Tip: A quick and accurate way to do this is to place all three boards together, centered on the cover paper. Remove the spine board, apply glue, and then place the spine board back in the slot between the two cover boards.

4. Press and rub with waxed paper.

5. Mark the hinge space on each side of the spine. The average hinge is two to three pieces of cardboard wide. See the technical notes at the end of the section to determine an exact measurement. *³⁄₁₆" (4.7 mm) from the spine*

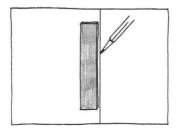

6. To glue on the front and back cover boards, apply glue to the back cover board. Center it head to tail, with the left edge to the line. *This will leave a ³⁄₁₆" (4.7 mm) hinge.* Press and rub with waxed paper. Follow the same steps to glue on the front cover board.

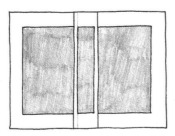

7. Trim the turn-ins so they are straight and equal widths. *½" (1.3 cm) on all sides*

8. Decide which kind of corner you will use. If making a library corner, stick down the corners. (See "How to Make a Library Corner," page 42.) If making a mitered corner, trim the corners. (See "How to Make a Mitered Corner," page 43.) The illustrations here show mitered corners.

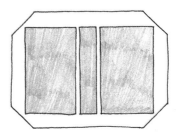

9. Glue the turn-ins in place. Apply glue to the turn-ins at the head and tail and fold them over the cover boards. Press and rub with waxed paper.

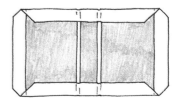

Glue down the turn-ins at the foredges following the same steps.

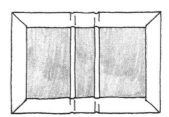

Technical note: The reason for first gluing the turn-ins at the head and tail is so that the little raised area at the corner will be on the edge of the boards, not the bottom. This way the book will stand perfectly level on the shelf and the raised area will not get scuffed as the book is slid in and out of the shelf.

Tip: Once you gain some confidence, you can use this faster way to make a case using paper or book cloth:

1. Apply glue to the cover material instead of the cardboard.

2. Position and press the spine and cover boards.

3. Trim the turn-ins and corners without measuring.

4. Press and rub with waxed paper.

Tip: If the scissor blades get loaded up with glue and don't cut as well, scrub the blades with a synthetic scrub pad in warm water to remove the glue.

STEP 6: PREPARE THE CASE

1. Fold the case around the bookblock.

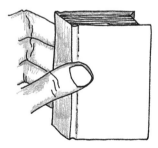

2. Wiggle the bookblock in the case until it fits snugly at the spine.

3. If you are using paper for the cover, it will probably not lay flat against the edge of the spine board.

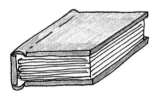

4. Flatten the cover paper to the edge of the spine board by rubbing with a bone folder. If you don't do this, the case will not fit the bookblock properly.

5. If the cover material is thick, the turn-ins may have created a depression on the inside of the case that needs to be filled. If necessary, fill the depression. (See step 5, "Apply a filler to the cover panel," page 47.)

STEP 7: GLUE THE BOOKBLOCK INTO THE CASE

1. Open the case with the turn-ins facing up.

2. With an awl, make small marks in the turn-ins to indicate the squares and where to place the foredge of the endpage. $\frac{1}{16}$" *(1.6 mm) from the edges*

3. Place the bookblock on the back cover of the case. Make sure it is oriented correctly.

4. Place scrap paper inside the front endpage to keep glue from getting on any other part of the bookblock.

5. Apply glue to the outside of the endpage.

6. Remove and discard the scrap paper.

7. Align the foredge and the head and tail of the endpage to the marks made inside the cover to indicate the square of the case.

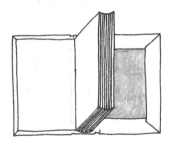

8. Press the endpage to the inside of the cover.

9. Rub with waxed paper, working from the foredge toward the spine.

10. Follow the same steps to glue the back endpage inside the back cover.

STEP 8: PRESS THE BOOK

1. Nestle the bookblock in the case. Make sure the spine of the bookblock fits snugly in the spine of the case.

2. Place waxed paper inside both endpages.

3. If this case has a groove in the hinge, gently press the cover material into the hinge with a bone folder. Use caution, because damp paper can be easily torn. Traditional binders press the book between boards that have a raised metal edge to accentuate a groove, but you can wrap rubber bands or string around the hinge to achieve the same goal.

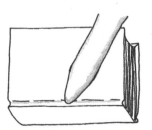

4.
Wrap waxed paper around the outside of the book.

5.
Place the book in a press, or under weights, and leave it to dry.

Technical notes: *How to calculate the exact dimensions of the cover boards and hinge*

1. The goal in making a case is to have it fit the bookblock snugly at the spine, foredge, head, and tail, with the desired square. If the hinge or boards are too wide, the case will be loose at the spine; if they are too narrow, the bookblock's foredge will be forced past the square.

2. To make exact calculations, begin with the dimensions of the bookblock and choose the width for the square. The average square is from ⅟₁₆" to ³⁄₁₆" (1.6 mm to 4.7 mm) wide, equal at the head, tail, and foredges, and in proportion to the size of the book.

3. The height of the cover boards should be equal to the height of the bookblock plus the width of the squares at the head and tail.

4. Variables for determining the width of the cover board and hinge include:

- If the cover boards are cut the same size as the bookblock, the spine, when cased in, will overhang the board by the width of the square. Thus, the hinge must be the width of the square plus the thickness of the spine board. If a case is made with these measurements, it will fit the bookblock perfectly, but usually the covers will not open flat because the hinge is not wide enough.

- To create a wider hinge, cut the covers slightly narrower than the bookblock and increase the hinge space proportionally. (Usually one board thickness.)

5. The width of the cover boards should be equal to the width of the bookblock less about one cardboard thickness; the width of the hinge should be the width of the square, plus the thickness of the spine board, plus about one cardboard thickness.

6. Even after following these steps there are still several other factors to consider to assure a perfect fit. If the cover material is thick, the hinge will need to be slightly larger.

If the cover material stretches, the hinge will need to be slightly smaller.

If the spine is rounded, the hinge will need to be made narrower.

If the cover material is pressed into the hinge to create a groove, and it cannot stretch, the hinge width will need to be increased.

THE PROJECTS
INTRODUCTION

This section of the book contains 12 step-by-step projects. These projects utilize the basic skills discussed in Section I, and we encourage you to refer back to them as needed. Each project describes a unique book structure. You may be familiar with some, others we have created and will be completely new. Each project specifies a certain set of measurements, but once you are familiar with the structure and how it is put together, you can alter the measurements to create a book of your own; the basic instructions apply to any size book.

One of the projects describes how to make books using found objects; for example, a ukulele or a camera. Finding ways to house your text pages within these unconventional object bindings will present unique challenges and have surprising solutions, but you will soon find the binding techniques are essentially the same as when making books with traditional cases and covers.

Another project presents the idea of altering books, and you will learn our "secret patented method" for creating a hollow cavity between the two covers of a book. This hollow book can then be used to house a text, a shrine, or any other kind of storytelling vehicle you want to create.

Each project will be followed by examples of different books we have made using the same binding or book structure. We hope these examples will expand your notion of how a book can be made and what a book can be or do, and that they will inspire you to experiment with the structure and make your own variations.

A word about miniature books:

Many of the projects in this book are small in scale. Miniature books have a long and grand history, and today there is a revival of interest in the format. Miniature books show up in every book arts exhibition, and most libraries have added them to their collections. There is even a Miniature Book Society with an annual meeting and book fair.

What is a miniature book? It is any book that measures less than 3" (7.6 cm) in every dimension. There are as many kinds of miniature books as there are books in general. For some, the challenge is to make the world's smallest book (the smallest so far is just under $\frac{1}{32}$" [1 mm] square). There are miniature books that replicate larger books on a small scale. Miniature books come leather-bound and paperback, with big type and with microscopic type, and with text on every subject imaginable. Miniature books are like jewelry, with words and images instead of gemstones, and wonderful binding materials instead of precious metals.

Why make miniature books? There are many reasons besides the intrigue of scale. Miniature books are inexpensive to produce. The materials can be scraps from other projects; flawed sections of marbled paper can look beautiful in a miniature book. Portions of old drawings or paintings can be used for covers or endpages, and scraps of mat board can be used for covers. Miniature books are also generally easier to make than larger books. The materials are easy to cut and, with little surface area, they are also easy to glue. Miniature books usually do not warp as they dry, so owning a big and heavy bookbinder's press is not a requirement. The only thing difficult about making miniature books is reading the ruler: miniature books require accurate, small measurements. A miniature book is the perfect literary vehicle for short texts—a favorite saying, a thought, a poem, or the fragment of a dream. Because miniature books usually have few words and are, by their nature, small, they can usually be completed in days or weeks rather than in months or years, which is often the case when making a larger book.

How to use this book:

We begin the bookmaking classes we teach by reminding participants not to worry about trying to make their best artwork—a *Mona Lisa* of the book world—in the class. We suggest they have fun, figure out how the binding is made, and consider their book a study for what they will do later on in their own studios. We suggest you approach the projects in this book with the same attitude: First make each project using scrap materials rather than precious artwork that has taken a long time to create. Follow the steps, gain an understanding of how the structure works, and then make the book again, this time with the finest materials, exploring the ideas and imagery inspired by the model book. Remember, you can easily change and adapt the measurements to make books of any size. Experiment, and have fun.

This project will familiarize you with the basic instructions for making a case-bound book. You can then use the same techniques, on a smaller scale, to make a dollhouse-size book and book jewelry. (The standard dollhouse in the USA is built on a 1" (2.5 cm) to 12" (30.5 cm) scale. This means the average book in a dollhouse is about ¾" (1.9 cm) tall.) We encourage you to increase the scale and make a bigger book. Experiment, develop new variations, and make as many books as possible. Remember, practice makes perfect.

Three blank case-bound books: a matchbook cover, a paste paper cover, and a cloth cover; and *Alphabet People*, 1989. 2⅜" x 1⅞" (6 cm x 4.7 cm), 64 pages. 200 copies.

Detail: *Alphabet People*.

Each letter of the alphabet is illustrated with a
sketch by Tanya Thomas (age 6) of what a person
would look like when forming the shape of the
letter with his or her body.

The project will describe how to case bind two different sizes of miniature books and then how to use those books to make jewelry. The miniature book will measure 2⅞" x 1⅞" (7.3 cm x 4.8 cm). The dollhouse-size book will measure ⅞" x ⅝" (2.2 cm x 1.6 cm).

The miniature multiple-section case-bound book
STEP 1:
PREPARE THE MATERIALS

1. Cut eight pieces of paper for the textblock, each measuring 2¾" x 3½" (7 cm x 8.9 cm), grain short.

2. Cut two pieces of paper for the endpages, each measuring 2¾" x 3½" (7 cm x 8.9 cm), grain short.

3. Cut two cover boards, each measuring 2⅞" x 1¹¹⁄₁₆" (7.3 cm x 4.3 cm), grain long.

4. Cut one spine board that is 2⅞" (7.3 cm) tall, grain long. The spine width will be the thickness of two cover boards plus the thickness of the bookblock. (See "How to Make a Case and Case-in a Bookblock," page 48.) The spine in our example measures 2⅞" x ⅜" (7.3 cm x 1 cm).

5. Cut one piece of paper to cover the case that measures 4" x 5¼" (10.2 cm x 13.3 cm), grain short.

STEP 2:
SEW THE TEXTBLOCK

Fold and sew the pages. (See "How to Sew Multiple Sections for a Miniature Textblock," page 34.)

Materials

- Paper for text (light weight)
- Paper for endpages (light weight)
- Paper for the cover (medium weight)
- Cardboard for the miniature book (medium weight)
- Cardboard for the cover boards and spine of the dollhouse-size book (light weight)
- Jewelry findings: tie tack and clutch (⁵⁄₁₆" [8 mm] or similar size) and pin back (¾" [1.9 cm] or equivalent)

STEP 3:
PREPARE THE TEXTBLOCK FOR BINDING

Glue the spine, then fold and attach the endpages. (See "How to Prepare the Textblock for Binding," steps 1 and 2, page 39.)

Technical note: We have not found it necessary to reinforce the hinge of a miniature book with a spine lining.

STEP 4:
MAKE THE CASE AND CASE-IN THE BOOKBLOCK

Glue the boards to the cover paper, leaving ³⁄₁₆" (4.7 mm) hinges. Make the corners, glue down the turn-ins, and case-in the bookblock. (See "How to Make a Case and Case-in a Bookblock," steps 5–8, page 50.)

Technical note: When pressing a miniature book in a press, place cardboard that is the same thickness as the finished book around the book to keep the book from being pressed too much and becoming squashed.

The dollhouse-size single-section case-bound book
STEP 1:
PREPARE THE MATERIALS

1. Cut five pieces of paper for the textblock, each measuring
¾" x 1" (1.9 cm x 2.5 cm), grain short.

2. Cut two pieces of paper for the endpages, each measuring
¾" x 1" (1.9 cm x 2.5 cm), grain short.

3. Cut two pieces of thin cardboard for the cover boards, each
measuring ⅞" x ½" (2.2 cm x 1.3 cm), grain long.

4. Cut one piece of thin cardboard for the spine that is ⅞"
(2.2 cm) tall, grain long. The spine width will be the thickness of
two cover boards plus the thickness of the bookblock. (See "How
to Make a Case and Case-in a Bookblock," step 2, page 49.)

5. Cut one piece of paper for the cover that measures 1⅜" x 2"
(3.5 x 5.1 cm), grain short. The turn-ins will be ¼" (0.6 cm),
and the hinges will be ⅛" (0.3 cm).

STEP 2:
SEW THE TEXTBLOCK

1. Fold the paper into ¾" x ½" (1.9 cm x 1.3 cm) folios. Make
one five-page section, and sew the section. (See "How to Sew
a Single-Section Textblock," page 32.)

2. Fold and attach the endpages flush to the foredge.

STEP 3:
MAKE THE CASE

Glue the boards to the cover paper, leaving ⅛" (0.3 cm)
hinges. Make the corners, and glue down the turn-ins. (See
"How to Make a Case and Case-in a Bookblock," page 48.)

STEP 4:
CASE-IN THE TEXTBLOCK

Glue the outer pages of the bookblock as if they were
endpages, inside the front and back covers. (See "How to
Make a Case and Case-in a Bookblock," step 7, page 51.)
Set the bookblock under weights to dry.

Dollhouse Books, 2004. ⅞" x ⅝" (2.2 cm x 1.6 cm).

Faux Dollhouse Books, 2004. ⅞" x ⅝"
(2.2 cm x 1.6 cm).

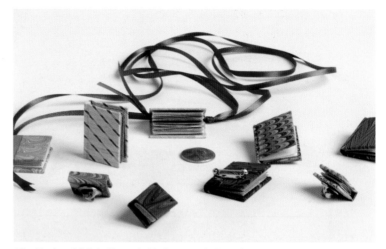

Tie Tacks, 2004, ⅞" x ⅝" (2.2 cm x 1.6 cm);
Book Pins, 2004, ⅞" x ⅝" (2.2 cm x 1.6 cm);
Book Necklaces, 2004, ⅞" x ⅝" (2.2 cm x 1.6 cm).

Dollhouse-size book with faux pages

To fill the shelves of a dollhouse, the bookblock can be a solid block instead of real pages. Just cut a piece of wood that measures ¾" x ½" (1.9 cm x 1.3 cm) or, alternatively, cut several pieces of cardboard that measure ¾" x ½" (1.9 cm x 1.3 cm), and glue them together. (They can be painted for further effect.) Glue this bookblock into a dollhouse case made as described on page 59.

The miniature book as jewelry

THE TIE TACK

Make the bookblock and case for a dollhouse-size book as described on page 59. Before casing-in the bookblock, poke a hole through the back cover with an awl. Apply glue to the post of a ⁵⁄₁₆" (0.8 cm) tie tack and insert it through the hole from the inside of the back cover. Then case-in the bookblock. The clutch will slip over the exposed post.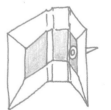

THE BOOK PIN

Make a miniature or dollhouse-size book, as described on page 59, that is at least ⅛" (0.3 cm) wider than the pin back. Glue the clip to the outside of the back cover, using silicone adhesive or epoxy. Small books can also be glued to barrettes or bolo ties.

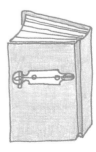

THE NECKLACE OR HANGING ORNAMENT

1. Make the bookblock for a miniature book.

2. Cut a piece of ⅛" (0.3 cm) ribbon that is 34" (86 cm) long.

3. Glue one end of the ribbon to the spine, leaving 2" (5.1 cm) extending below the tail of the bookblock. ●➤

4. Place the other end of the ribbon in the valley, leaving 2" (5.1 cm) extending below the tail of the bookblock. ●➤

5. Tie the ends of the ribbon below the tail of the bookblock in a knot, and tie another knot above the head of the bookblock. ●➤

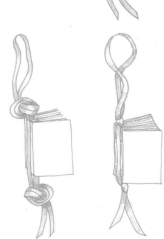

6. Glue the bookblock into the case.

7. When dry, the book will hang from the ribbon.

8. The size of the book can be varied; multiple books can be hung together; and string, leather, or chain can be used in place of ribbon.

Dressing Dilemma, 1999. 2¾" x 2⅛" (7 cm x 5.4 cm). Watercolor illustration of dresses on cutout pages and handwritten text by Donna Thomas. Bound in red leather with a blue dress leather onlay on the cover.

The simplest way to make an accordion book is to fold paper back and forth and use the outer pages as covers. However, what is simple is not always elegant, sturdy, or worth much further investment. By attaching hard covers and by adding text, illustration, color, and texture to the interior pages, you will create a book that is more than just a structure: it will be a work of art.

The following project describes an interesting variation on the simple accordion book, one we developed to bring with us when we travel. Before beginning the project, take an opportunity to become familiar with the accordion structure. Follow the steps given in "How to Fold an Accordion," (see page 24) and "How to Make Panel Covers and Attach an Accordion," (see page 45). Try making a number of accordion books in different sizes and shapes until the steps are second nature; then making this book will be easy.

My Dad's Desk, 2003.
2¹¹⁄₁₆" x 2³⁄₁₆" (6.8 cm x 5.6 cm).
A few old pencils from Donna's dad's desk inspired the creation of this book. There is no written text; watercolor illustrations, painted on yellow handmade paper, and the small objects in the pockets tell the story.

The dimensions of this book will be 2⅝" x 2⅛" (6.7 cm x 5.4 cm). The book uses a variation of the simple accordion described in "How to Fold an Accordion" (see page 24), which has eight pages, each with a pocket.

STEP 1:

MAKE THE ACCORDION

1. Cut paper for the accordion that measures 6½" x 16" (16.5 cm x 40.6 cm), grain short.

2. Fold the sheet into a 6½" x 2" (16.5 cm x 5.1 cm) eight-page accordion. (See "How to Fold an Accordion," page 24.)

STEP 2:

FOLD THE POCKETS

1. Open the accordion out flat on a cutting mat.

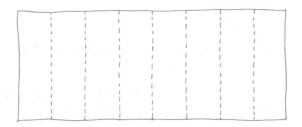

2. Make marks at each end of the accordion that are ½" (1.3 cm), 1¾" (4.4 cm), and 4¼" (10.8 cm) from the bottom.

Materials

- Paper for the accordion (medium to heavy weight)
- Cardboard (medium weight)
- Paper for the cover (light to medium weight)

3. Make horizontal scored lines between these marks. The scores will be perpendicular to the accordion folds.

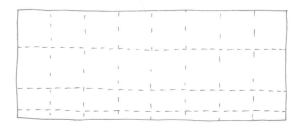

4. Make a valley fold at the ½" (1.3 cm) score, and crease it flat.

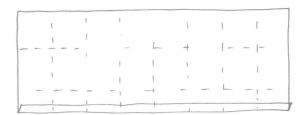

5. Make a valley fold at the 4¼" (10.8 cm) score, and crease it flat.

6. Make a valley fold at the 1¾" (4.4 cm) score, and crease it flat to complete the pockets.

7. Refold along the original accordion folds made in step 1. This will produce a 2½" x 2" (6.4 cm x 5.1 cm) bookblock with eight accordion pages, each with a pocket at the bottom.

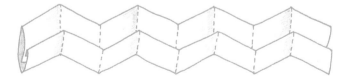

8. Place a dab of glue inside the pocket at each mountain and valley fold, as well as at the foredges, to hold the pockets together.

Tip: The pockets can also be sewn together at the folds and ends.

9. Place under weight to dry while making the covers.

STEP 3:
MAKE THE PANEL COVERS

1. Cut two cover boards, each measuring 2⅝" x 2⅛" (6.7 cm x 5.4 cm), grain long.

2. Cut two pieces of cover material, each measuring 3⅝" x 3⅛" (9.2 cm x 7.9 cm).

3. Make the two cover panels. (See steps 4 and 5, "How to Make Panel Covers and Attach an Accordion," page 45.)

STEP 4:
ASSEMBLE THE BOOK

1. If there is any artwork or writing, be sure to orient the front cover to the front of the bookblock.

2. Glue the outside of the accordion's first page to the front cover. (See "How to Make Panel Covers and Attach an Accordion," step 6, page 47.)

3. Repeat step 2 to glue the outside of the back page to the back cover.

4. Press to dry by placing separate weights on each cover. When the book is dry, decorate the pages and place items in the pockets. We take blank pocket accordion books to collage and paint while we are on trips. We use the pockets for saving mementos.

Loket, 1999. 2 ¹¹⁄₁₆" x 2 ³⁄₁₆" (6.8 cm x 5.6 cm). A trip to the scenic
Czech village of Loket was documented in this book. Sketches of
Loket were made on the pockets and covers; photos and ephemera
were placed in the pockets.

The Trout, 2003. 2⅝" x 2¼" (6.7 cm x 5.7 cm). Illustrations of trout and the lakes where they were caught document a Sierra fishing trip. A quote from Shakespeare's *Twelfth Night*, "Here comes the trout that must be caught by tickling" is on a separate accordion in front. To tickle a trout is to poach it, or catch it with your hands, and we have seen some of that go on in the backcountry. The flies we used dangle from threads and can be "fished out" of the pockets. The covers are blue leather, and an onlay of a trout is on the front. The slipcase is covered with Peggy Skycraft's marbled paper with a pocket title label on the front.

We began our work as traditional craftspeople making blank books and handmade paper. We then became printers and learned to make fine-press books. At that time the book was a simple and easily understood concept; it was archetypal, a thing like the Gutenberg Bible, a monumental text in a beautiful and sturdy binding. This may explain why it was so long before we made our first accordion-fold book. The format seemed too ephemeral, anathema to a more formal aesthetic. This may also explain why, when we did start to make accordion books, we tried to make them conform to our picture of a book by forcing them into bindings. These attempts to contain the accordion were successful, and they led to the creation of the case-bound fold-out accordion described in this project.

This book combines the formal structure of the case-bound book and the freedom of the accordion format. The project demonstrates how basic book structures (as described in the "How To" section) can be used as building blocks to create new book structures. In this book, the accordion pages are wrapped by a case but are attached only inside the back cover. The front of the accordion is attached to a separate panel, which serves to decorate the piece and to give the reader something to hold on to when opening the book.

In Love, 2004. 2¾" x 1¾" (7 cm x 4.4 cm). The 10 accordion pages are cut like a paper doll chain, each hand painted as a different person, with a Hawaiian proverb, "Be one in love. I ho'okahi ka umauma, ho'okahi ke aloha.", in both English and Hawaiian, in a banner running the length of the accordion. The blue cover is handmade paper and the inside cover papers are Japanese printed papers.

The book will measure 2¾" x 1¾" (7 cm x 4.4 cm). The eight-page accordion will be cut into shapes, like a paper doll chain, and then glued to both a case and a panel cover.

STEP 1:
MAKE THE ACCORDION

1. Cut paper for the accordion that measures 2½" x 12" (6.4 cm x 30.5 cm), grain short.

2. Fold the paper into an eight-page accordion. Each page will measure 2½" x 1½" (6.4 cm x 3.8 cm). (See "How to Fold an Accordion," page 24.)

STEP 2:
CUT THE SHAPED ACCORDION

1. Cut paper for a template that measures 2½" x 1½" (6.4 cm x 3.8 cm).

2. Design and cut out the shape of the template paper. To create a symmetrical pattern, fold the template in half and draw half of the image. Be sure to leave paper at both mountain and valley folds so the accordion stays connected.

3. Place the template on the first page of the accordion, and trace around it with a pencil.

4. Cut out the shape using scissors or a sharp utility knife.

5. Cut through all layers of the accordion to create the shaped chain.

Materials

- Paper for the accordion (medium weight and strong)
- Paper for the cover of the panel and case (medium weight)
- Paper for the inside of the panel and case (light to medium weight)
- Cardboard for the panel and case (medium weight)

STEP 3:
MAKE THE PANEL COVER

1. Cut one piece of cardboard for the panel board that measures 2⅝" x 1⅝" (6.7 cm x 4.1 cm), grain long. ¹⁄₁₆" *(1.6 mm) squares*

2. Cut one piece of paper to cover the panel board that measures 3⅝" x 2⅝" (9.2 cm x 6.7 cm), grain long.

3. Cut one piece of paper to cover the inside of the panel (the inside cover paper) that measures 2½" x 1½" (6.4 cm x 3.8 cm), grain long.

4. Glue the panel board to the cover paper and make the panel. (See "How to Make Panel Covers and Attach an Accordion," page 47.)

5. Glue the inside cover paper, centered on the squares, to the inside of the panel.

6. Press and rub with waxed paper.

7. Place under weight to dry.

STEP 4:
MAKE THE CASE

1. Cut two cover boards, each measuring 2¾" x 1⅝" (7 cm x 4.1 cm), grain long. ⅛" *(0.3 cm) squares*

2. Cut one spine board that is 2¾" (7 cm) high. The width of the spine will equal the thickness of the two cover boards and the panel cover, plus the thickness of the bookblock. The spine of our example book measures 2¾" x ⁵⁄₁₆" (7 cm x 0.8 cm), grain long.

3. Cut one piece of paper to cover the case that measures 3½" x 4¾" (8.9 cm x 12.1 cm), grain short.

4. Glue the spine and cover boards to the cover paper and make the case. (See "How to Make a Case and Case-in a Bookblock," step 5, page 49.)

5. Measure and cut one piece of paper for the inside cover that measures 2⅝" x about 3⅞" (6.7 cm x 9.8 cm), grain short. Make all the squares equal. The width of the inside cover paper will vary depending on the width of the hinges.

6. Apply glue to the inside cover paper and place it centered on the inside of the case.

Press and rub with waxed paper. Press the inside cover paper slightly into the grooves on both sides of the spine.

7. Leave under weights to dry.

STEP 5:
GLUE THE SHAPED ACCORDION BOOKBLOCK TO THE PANEL COVER AND CASE

1. Fold the case around the panel and bookblock, and rub the cover paper flush against the edges of the spine board. (See "How to Make a Case and Case-in a Bookblock," step 6, page 51.)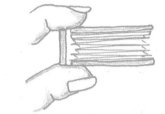

2. Open the case, remove the accordion, and orient it so the end folds are valley folds. Glue the accordion's first page, centered, on the inside of the panel cover. This will create ¹⁄₁₆" (1.6 mm) squares. Press and rub with waxed paper.

Glue the accordion's last page, centered, inside the back cover of the case. This will create ⅛" (0.3 cm) squares. They will not line up with the edges of the inside cover paper. Press and rub with waxed paper.

3. Place under weight to dry.

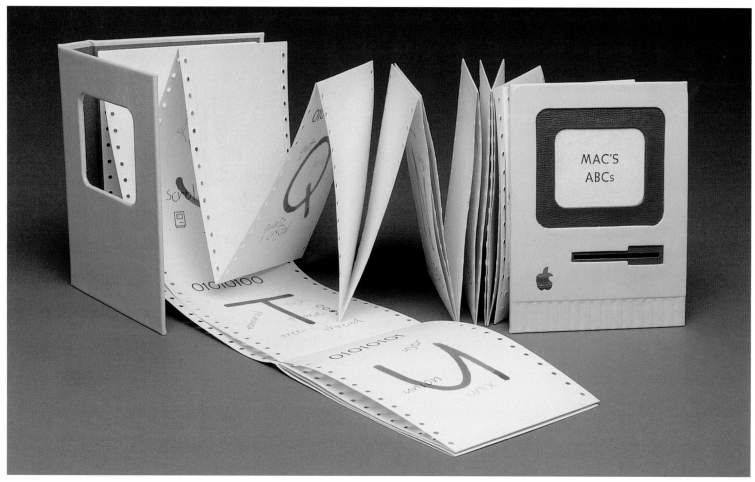

Mac's ABCs, 1996. 7¼" x 5½" (18.5 cm x 14 cm).

Imagining that a time will come when computers get so fast that they will run out of things to do, we decided they would probably take up reading to fill their spare time. Young computers will need to have "children's books," and anticipating this need, we created this binary ABC book to help them learn to read. The A's, B's, and C's are all in 1's and 0's; 01000001 is A, 01000010 is B, and so on. Each page is illustrated with a calligraphic rendering of the letter. We imagine young computers will scan these images to discover the visual representation of the binary digits. It is not much harder to imagine that *Mac's ABCs*, along with the other books we might create (like *DOS and Mac*: "Look Mac. See DOS. DOS can run. Run, Windows, run."), will become classics of the genre, and that some day in the future these books will be found on every virtual bookshelf in the world.

The leather binding was made to resemble a computer, with leather onlays to create the disk drive, logo, and black monitor rim. The monitor's screen is made from sheepskin parchment, and the title was letterpress printed. The paper was hand made and perforated to resemble computer paper. The text was letterpress printed and illustrations were hand painted.

Accordion to Zither: A Musical ABC, 2002. 2⅜" x 1⅞" (6.1 cm x 4.7 cm). This alphabet book presents 26 favorite musical instruments in watercolor illustrations. This book has 30 accordion pages copied in color on handmade paper. The open case binding is covered in hand-drawn sheet music. 100 copies.

Climb the Mountains, 1995. 2⅝" x 1⅞" (6.7 cm x 4.7 cm). The text is a quote by John Muir. The 17 accordion-folded pages of lettering and illustration are printed from carved linoleum blocks. The unique paper was hand made; colored pulps were painted onto the surface to create the background for the earth, sky, and trees. The handmade paper binding is folded from a single sheet of paper and has the front, back, and spine covered with wooden veneer from trees that grow in the Sierra Nevada mountain range. 100 copies. Also shown, *The John Muir Trail*, 2000. 2⅜" x 1¾ (6 cm x 4.4 cm), which features a ribbon closure.

Early American Chairs, 1997. 2½" x 1⅜" (6.4 cm x 3.5 cm). An accordion-folded paper chain, with 12 individually cut-out watercolor paintings of chairs, illustrates a quote from Henry David Thoreau's *Walden*: "I had three chairs in my house: one for solitude, two for friendship, and three for society."

Many artists use layering as a way to add interest and complexity to their work. Accordions can be layered, or nested, to make interesting artists' books. The technique is employed to make "star" or "carousel" books with layers of the inner accordions cut away to create three-dimensional pages, as can be seen in our *Golden Gate Bridge* (see page 80). We were exploring this concept when we saw *River of Stars*, a book with an interlocking accordion made by Julie Chen and Ed Hutchins. Their structure inspired us to create something similar. We imagined a number of different possibilities, then created several prototypes before developing this simple and elegant system to make a nested accordion book with pop-up-like motion.

Song of Creation, 1999. 2⅝" x 2⅛" (6.7 cm x 5.4 cm). The text is a quote by John Muir. "From form to form, beauty to beauty, ever changing never resting, all are speeding with love's enthusiasm, singing with the stars the eternal song of creation." The illustration, originally a watercolor painting that was color copied for this book, pays homage to creation: a 180-degree panorama of the awe-inspiring granite mountains that make up the Yosemite Valley.

This book will measure 2⅞" x 1⅞" (7.3 cm x 4.7 cm). The bookblock will measure 2¾" x 1¾" (7 cm x 4.4 cm). The basic idea of this structure is to nest a smaller and shorter accordion into a larger and longer accordion. The outer accordion has 10 pages and the inner accordion has 8. The number of pages can vary, but the principle remains the same: The outside accordion must always be at least two pages longer than the inside one. There will be four 2" x 1¾" (5.1 cm x 4.4 cm) pop-ups on the outer accordion, but the word "pop-up" is sort of misleading; these panels will actually pop back.

STEP 1:
MAKE THE EIGHT-PAGE INNER ACCORDION
1. Cut one piece of paper for the inner accordion that measures 2" x 14" (5.1 cm x 35.6 cm), grain short.

2. Fold into an eight-page accordion. (See "How to Fold an Accordion," page 24.)

STEP 2:
MAKE THE TEN-PAGE OUTER ACCORDION
1. Cut one piece of paper for the outer accordion that measures 2¾" x 17½" (7 cm x 44.5 cm), grain short.

2. Mark 14" (35.6 cm) from the left edge.

3. Make a fold.

4. Ignore the 3½" (8.9 cm) length of the paper.

5. Fold the 14" (35.6 cm) length into a four-page accordion. (See "How to Fold an Accordion," page 24.) Each of the four pages will measure 3½" (8.9 cm), so there will now be a total of five 3½" (8.9 cm) pages.

Materials
- Paper for accordions (medium to heavy weight)
- Cover material (light to medium weight)
- Cardboard (medium weight)

6. Reverse all folds so that there are only mountain folds.

7. Fold the five pages to create a 10-page accordion. (See "How to Fold an Accordion", page 24.)

STEP 3:
CUT AND SCORE THE POP-UPS IN THE OUTER ACCORDION
1. Fold the two endpages of the outer accordion back to the left so they do not get cut in the steps that follow.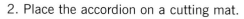

2. Place the accordion on a cutting mat.

3. Make two small marks with an awl at the right foredge, one ⅜" (1 cm) from the head and the other ⅜" (1 cm) from the tail.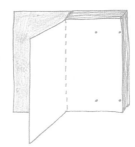

4. Make two more marks in the center of the page, one ⅜"
(1 cm) from the head and the other ⅜" (1 cm) from the tail.

These holes must go through all the accordion layers.

The marks must be parallel to the foredge, and there must be
2" (5.1 cm) between the marks for the inner accordion to fit.
The accordion page is 1¾" (4.4 cm) wide, so these marks are
⅞" (2.2 cm) from the foredge.

5. Draw a horizontal line between the mark at the center and
the corresponding mark at the foredge. Do this at both the
head and the tail of the book.

6. Cut along the line, from the center to the foredge, through
all layers of the accordion.

To do this, hold the work firmly and do not try to cut through
all the layers in one cut. Make multiple light cuts.

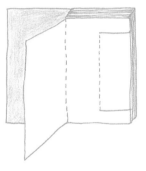

7. Make a vertical scored line between the two marks in the
center of each page.

STEP 4:
FOLD THE POP-UPS BACK

1. Open up the accordion.

2. Four 2" x 1¾" (5.1 cm x 4.4 cm) rectangles, each spanning
two accordion pages, have been created by the cuts and
scores just made. These will be the pop-up pages.

3. Reverse the mountain folds of each rectangle, and lightly
crease along the score lines at each end of the rectangle to
define the pop-up pages.

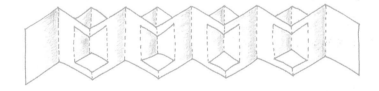

4. Crease each fold flat, making sure that the valley folds align
perfectly along the spine.

5. Leave the ⅜" (1 cm) folds at the head and tail of the
outer accordion (these are above and below the rectangles)
as mountain folds.

STEP 5:
NEST THE INNER AND OUTER ACCORDIONS

1. Place the four valleys of the inner accordion into the four popped-back valleys of the outer accordion. Make sure they nest together snugly, then remove the inner accordion.

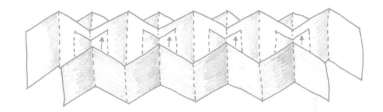

2. Apply glue to each popped-back valley of the outer accordion. Do not glue the entire rectangle, because too much glue will cause the pages to warp. A dab in the valley fold is sufficient to hold them together.

3. Carefully position the valley folds of the inner accordion in the glued valleys of the outer accordion.

4. Press and rub with waxed paper.

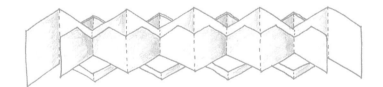

STEP 6:
MAKE THE PANEL COVERS AND GLUE IN THE BOOKBLOCK

1. Cut two cover boards that each measure 2⅞" x 1⅞" (7.3 cm x 4.8 cm), grain long.

2. Cut two pieces of cover material that each measure 3⅞" x 2⅞" (9.8 cm x 7.3 cm), grain long.

3. Make the two cover panels. (See "How to Make Panel Covers and Attach an Accordion," step 4, page 46.)

4. Glue the front and back covers to the accordion bookblock. (See "How to Make Panel Covers and Attach an Accordion," steps 5–6, page 47.) Make sure the bookblock and covers are oriented correctly. Place the book under weights to dry.

This is a great book structure to take on trips. We make the outer accordion and attach the covers before leaving. Then we decorate and attach the inner accordion while we are traveling.

Home on the Range, 2001. 3" x 2" (7.6 cm x 5.1 cm). Handmade paper was folded into an accordion, cut to the desired shape, and then hand painted. The front panel is covered with leather, and the image is a leather onlay.

Stars, 2000. 2⅞" x 2⅛" (7.3 cm x 5.4 cm). The text is a quote by R. W. Emerson, from *Nature*, which begins, "But if a man would be alone, let him look at the stars." The illustrations have stars made with embroidered French knots of metallic gold thread and painted lines that connect the constellations. The cover panels are made with dark blue leather. The silhouette of the Little Dipper is set in rhinestones on the front cover. The book is housed in a marbled paper–covered slipcase.

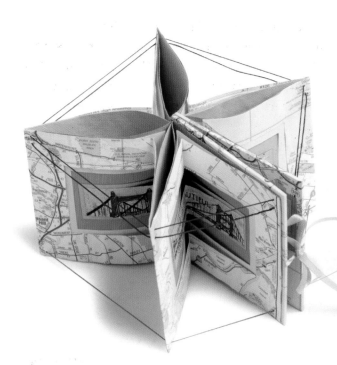

Golden Gate Bridge, 2003. (7.3 cm x 6.7 cm). This book commemorates the place the Golden Gate Bridge has in Donna's life: her grandpa helped build it, her dad commuted across it, and everyone has marveled at its beauty. The book uses string to mimic the cables of the bridge. The ribbon ties can hold it open as a "star" book.

Button, 1998. 1¹¹⁄₁₆" x 1¹⁵⁄₁₆" (4.3 cm x 4.9 cm).
This book features quotes with the word button in them by
Robert Burns, Lewis Carroll, and William Shakespeare. The
text was hand written and buttons from Donna's button
collection were sewn on the pop-up inner accordion as
illustrations. The book was case bound in blue Moroccan
leather and three buttons have been inset on the front cover.

The Red Dog, 1992. 1⅜" x 1³⁄₁₆" (3.5 cm x 2.0 mm). The text,
written by Tanya Thomas and illustrated by Suzanne Thomas, was
letterpress printed from metal type and linoleum cuts. Illustrations
are hand colored. The panel covers are wrapped with marbled paper.
A black leather "dog collar" holds the book closed.

We developed the accordion pleat spine stab-sewn structure, described in this project, to bind together 35 different kinds of handmade paper for our book *Paper from Plants* (see page 88). Each 8½" x 11" (21.6 cm x 27.9 cm) sheet was made from a different plant, and each varied in weight, texture, and flexibility. The number of papers that were thick and inflexible ruled out the use of a traditional stab binding. Traditional sewing systems were not going to work because some papers could not be folded, nor could they be guarded or glued into folios because of their incompatibility or dimensional instability.

We decided that an accordion structure, like the one we had used for an earlier book, *Girls* (see page 89), might be a solution, especially if we sewed the papers to the accordion instead of using glue. We made a model but, because of the larger scale, it proved unmanageable. Making more models, we discovered that pages could be stab sewn between two adjacent pleats to create a series of stab bindings along the spine. The pleated spine gave a flexibility not usually associated with stab binding, and it also created space for thick and cockled papers. It even produced a stab-sewn book that stayed open when on display. It was a perfect solution, and it has become a good structure to use any time we are binding single sheets of paper.

The binding we describe is a three-part case, a simple variation of the standard case binding that we thought we had invented. That was until the first bookbinder we showed it to told us, "I teach it in my first-year classes." There really is nothing new under the sun, and it is possible that some other book artist has also invented each binding structure we describe in this book.

Fight for California, 2004. 4¼" x 5¼" (10.8 cm x 13.3 cm), cover view. The text is the University of California at Berkeley's "fight song," and the photos are of the university's 2004 marching band. The three-part binding has a leather spine and "cloud" handmade paper on the covers. Also shown: *The Luck*, 2004. 4¼" x 5¼" (10.8 cm x 13.3 cm), interior view. A quote from Brett Hart's *The Luck of Roaring Camp*, "Tell the boys I've got the luck with me now," is handwritten over cards that are sewn to pages on an accordion-pleat spine. The endpages are antique marbled paper made in the time of the gold rush, and the three-part binding has the same marbled paper for the spine and handmade paper for the covers.

This book will measure 4¼" x 5½" (10.8 cm x 14 cm). The pleated spine bookblock has six stab-sewn sections and is case bound in a three-part case. The case is made by attaching cover panels to a spine panel.

STEP 1:

MAKE THE ACCORDION PLEAT SPINE

1. Cut one piece of paper for the accordion that measures 4" x 16" (10.2 cm x 40.6 cm), grain short.

2. Fold the accordion to make a thirty two-page accordion. Each page will be ½" (1.3 cm) wide. (See "How to Fold an Accordion," page 24.)

3. Cut off six pages to make a twenty six-page accordion.

4. Orient the accordion so that the endpages point up and the last folds are valley folds.

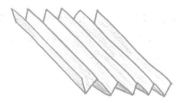

5. The endpages will not be marked, so fold them out of the way.

6. Mark three sewing stations on the accordion.

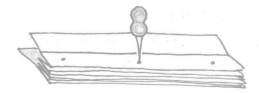

Materials

- Paper for the accordion pleat (strong)
- Paper for text (any weight)
- Paper for divider pages (medium weight)
- Photographs
- Paper for endpages and inside cover paper (medium weight)
- Cardboard (medium weight)
- Paper for covering the boards (medium weight)
- Cloth, paper, or leather for covering the spine (medium weight)

Mark station A ½" (1.3 cm) from the head. Mark station C ½" (1.3 cm) from the tail. Mark station B centered between the other two. The stations should be in the center of the pages.

7. Use an awl to pre-poke the sewing stations.

STEP 2:

PREPARE THE MATERIALS FOR THE ACCORDION PLEAT BOOKBLOCK

1. Cut five pieces of paper for the text that measure 3½" x 5" (8.9 cm x 12.7 cm), grain short.

2. Cut five photographs to accompany the text, each measuring 3½" x 5" (8.9 cm x 12.7 cm).

3. Cut six sheets of paper as divider pages to place between the photos and the text, each measuring 4" x 5¼" (10.2 cm x 13.3 cm), grain short.

4. Cut four sheets of the same paper as endpages, two to be sewn in the first and last sections, and two to be attached to the ends of the pleat. These sheets should measure 4" x 5¼" (10.2 cm x 13.3 cm), grain short.

STEP 3:
MAKE THE ACCORDION PLEAT BOOKBLOCK

1. Assemble the pages for section 1 as follows: endpage, divider page, photo.

2. Place section 1 in the second valley fold, between the first two mountain folds of the accordion pleat spine. ●➤

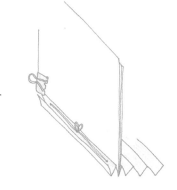

3. Place binder clips on the mountain folds at the head and tail of the accordion to hold the pages in place.

4. Cut a 12" (30.5 cm) length of thread. Stab sew through the pre poked stations using the pamphlet stitch. (See "How to Sew a Single-Section Textblock," page 32.) Sew through both pleats and the pages at the same time.

5. Follow steps 2–4 to sew sections 2–6 in place. Order the rest of the pages as follows:

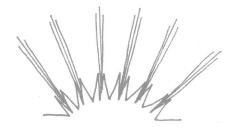

Sections 2–5: text, divider page, photo. Section 6: text, divider page, endpage.

6. Attach the endpages to the inside of the first and last accordion pleat. Apply glue to the inside of the front accordion pleat. Place one endpage into the bottom of the first valley, and press it to the accordion pleat.

7. Repeat step 6 to attach the back endpage inside the last accordion pleat.

Technical note: The page order can be varied. The only things that are fixed: section 1 must start with an endpage, and section 6 must end with an endpage.

STEP 4:
PREPARE THE MATERIALS FOR THE THREE-PART CASE

1. Cut two pieces of cardboard for the panel cover boards that measure 4¼" x 5¼" (10.8 cm x 13.3 cm), grain short. This book will have ⅛" (0.3 cm) squares.

2. Cut two pieces of paper to cover the boards, each measuring 5¼" x 6" (13.3 cm x 15.2 cm), grain short.

3. Cut one piece of cardboard for the spine panel board that is 4¼" (10.8 cm) high. The width will be the thickness of the two cover boards plus the thickness of the pleat spine bookblock. (See "How to Make a Case and Case-in a Bookblock," step 2, page 49.) The spine board for our book measures 4¼" x ⁹⁄₁₆" (10.8 cm x 1.4 cm), grain long.

4. Cut a piece of paper, cloth, or leather to cover the spine that measures 5¼" x 1¾" (13.3 cm x 4.4 cm), grain long.

STEP 5:
MAKE THE SPINE PANEL AND THE COVER PANELS

1. Place the spine cover material facedown.

2. Apply glue to the spine board and place it, centered, on the spine panel's cover material.

3. Press and rub with waxed paper.

4. Apply glue to the turn-ins at both the head and the tail.

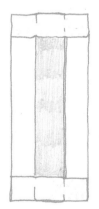

5. Fold the turn-ins straight over, and press them both to the inside of the spine board and along the inside of the spine material. ●◆

6. Press and rub with waxed paper.

7. Apply a thin layer of glue to the edges of the spine board. ●◆

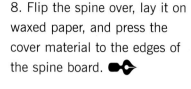
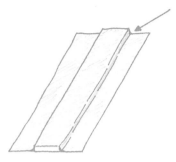

8. Flip the spine over, lay it on waxed paper, and press the cover material to the edges of the spine board. ●◆

9. Make the two panel covers. (See "How to Make Panel Covers and Attach an Accordion," step 4–6, page 46.)

STEP 6:
MAKE THE CASE

1. Place the spine panel faceup (turn-ins down).

2. Apply glue to the inside of the front panel cover (the end that will be near the spine). The glue should cover about ½" (1.3 cm) from the edge.

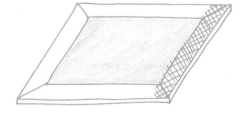

3. Align head to tail, and place the panel cover faceup on the spine panel, ³⁄₁₆" (4.7 mm) to the right of the spine board. The ³⁄₁₆" (4.7 mm) between the edge of the cover board and the edge of the spine board will create a hinge.

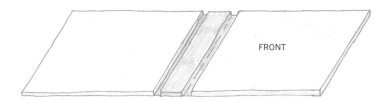

Tip: A ³⁄₁₆"- (4.7 mm-) wide strip of cardboard can be cut and placed between the cover board and the spine board to ensure proper hinge spacing.

4. Press and rub with waxed paper.

5. Repeat steps 2–4 to attach the back cover.

6. Place under weights or in a press to dry.

STEP 7:
CASE-IN THE ACCORDION PLEAT BOOKBLOCK

1. Place the case facedown, with the front cover to the left.

2. Place a piece of scrap paper in the valley between the endpage and the last sewn section.

3. Apply glue to the outside of the last endpage, then discard the scrap paper.

4. Check that the cover and bookblock are oriented correctly.

5. Place the last endpage inside the back cover, leaving ⅛" (0.3 cm) squares at the head, tail, and foredge.

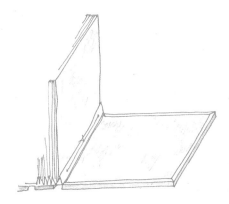

6. Press and rub with waxed paper.

7. Repeat these steps and glue the front endpage to the front cover.

STEP 8:
PRESS THE BOOK

1. Wrap the covers with waxed paper and place them under weights. To avoid crushing the pleated spine, the bookblock must not be pressed.

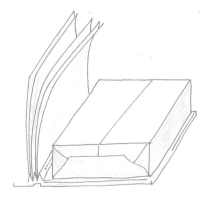

Technical note: This binding can also be used with a sewn bookblock.

 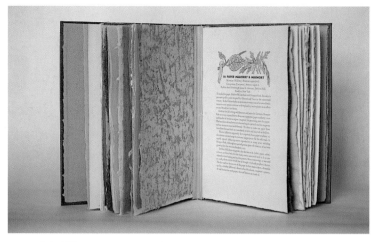

Paper from Plants, 1999. 11⅝" x 8¾" (29.5 cm x 22.2 cm). This book features 30 different paper specimens that have been handmade from local plants. Each plant is illustrated with a line drawing by Donna Thomas and text written by the papermaker. The text, sewn to an accordion-pleat spine, was letterpress printed on handmade paper. The three-part binding is made with green Moroccan leather and painted handmade paper. 100 pages. 120 copies.

The Tarantella Rose, 1995. 10⅝" x 7⅝" (27 cm x 19.4 cm). Previously unpublished poems by William Everson with seven linoleum-cut illustrations. Letterpress printed with Weiss type on handmade paper. This is one of seven special copies that are bound in a three-part binding using red Moroccan leather and origami-folded handmade paper made by Peter, designed and folded by Chris Palmer. 38 pages. 75 copies.

Girls, 1993. 2" x 1⅞" (5.1 cm x 4.7 cm). Suzanne and Tanya Thomas made 12 paintings of girls, originally to use for a card game while camping. These cards were later attached to a pink accordion pleat spine and bound in a yellow nonadhesive binding. The book is housed in a nonadhesive paper slipcase with the title cut out of the paper. 2 copies.

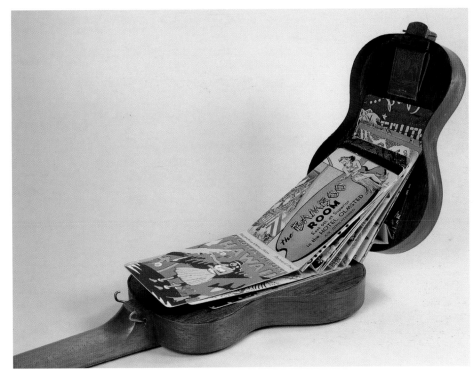

The Concertina Ukulele, 2002. 16" x 6" x 3" (40.6 cm x 15.2 cm x 7.6 cm). This ukulele was cut in half and boards were mounted inside the halves to create a cavity. The halves are hinged at the bottom of the ukulele, and there is a simple clasp through the heel. Cards with vintage images (from matchbooks and other Hawaiian ephemera) are attached to a paper pleat inside the ukulele. Two vintage matchbooks are mounted above and below the concertina.

Most commercial books have text printed on both sides of the page. The question that often arises for the artist is, "How can a book be made with paper that is printed or decorated on only one side?" The accordion is a common solution. Ancient models can be adapted to provide other solutions. The bamboo blind or Venetian blind books of Indonesia are bound by running string through holes in the pages. The palm leaf books of Southeast Asia bind single sheets, either at one end or the center, to create a fan. Many Asian stab bindings often use paper printed on one side: The paper is folded, printed side out, and sewn with the foredges in the spine. Western bindings also can be made with paper printed on only one side: The paper is folded in half twice, first vertically, then horizontally, keeping the printed side out, and is then sewn through the fold.

In 1990, we made a miniature book titled *Bayad* (see page 99). This book was photocopied onto Peter's handmade paper. We did not print on the back of the paper because a photocopy machine cannot produce front and back pages that are in exact registration. To best feature this one-sided page—and to honor the Asian heritage of the Philippines—we decided to make a book with a stab-sewn bookblock. We also letterpress printed illustrations on business card–size pieces of handmade paper that we had purchased from a hand paper mill in the Philippines. These cards were too stiff to use in a stab binding, so we developed the idea of a case-bound portfolio as a way to integrate these two different elements into one book. The stab-sewn text was held inside the back cover by sliding the last page under a glued-down paper band; the illustrations were attached inside the front cover with ribbon ties. Further exploration of this idea led to the creation of the case-bound pocket book, which is described in this project.

Need a Light?, 2003. 3" x 2¼" (7.6 cm x 5.7 cm). Matchbooks were color copied, and that paper was used for both the text and the cover. Matches have been inserted into the pocket to make this a real matchbook.

This book will measure 7¼" x 5¼" (18.4 cm x 13.3 cm). The bookblock is the same dimensions as the one described in "How to Make a Four-Hole Stab-Sewn Textblock" (see page 29). Pockets inside each cover will hold the bookblock and ephemera.

STEP 1:
MAKE THE BOOKBLOCK

1. Cut paper for the text that measures 7" x 5" (17.8 cm x 12.7 cm), grain long.

2. Cut a stiff paper backing the same size, 7" x 5" (17.8 cm x 12.7 cm), grain long.

3. Stack text pages on top of the stiff paper backing, and clamp them together with binder clips. ●◄

4. Mark sewing stations and stab sew the textblock. (See "How to Make a Four-Hole Stab-Sewn Textblock," page 29.)

Technical note: Stab sewing requires that the pages have large inner margins, so it is important that the text and illustrations are not too close to the spine.

STEP 2:
PREPARE THE MATERIALS FOR THE CASE

1. Cut two cover boards, each measuring 7¼" x 5" (18.4 cm x 12.7 cm), grain long.

2. Cut one spine board that measures 7¼" (18.4 cm) high, grain long. The spine width will be the thickness of two cover boards plus the thickness of two pieces of cover paper (the pockets), the thickness of the bookblock, and the thickness of the ephemera. The spine board for our book measured 7" x ½" (17.8 cm x 1.3 cm), grain long. (See "How to Make

Materials

- Paper for text (very light to light weight)
- Stiff paper backing (heavy weight)
- Cardboard (medium to heavy weight)
- Paper for cover (light to medium weight)
- Paper for inside cover paper (light to medium weight)
- Ephemera to put in pocket

a Case and Case-in a Bookblock," step 2, page 49.)

3. Cut one piece of paper for the cover that measures 8¼" x 18" (21 cm x 45.7 cm), grain short.

Technical note: The width of the cover paper includes 2½" (6.4 cm) for the ephemera pocket; 4½" (11.4 cm) for the pocket to hold the bookblock; and 11" (27.9 cm) for the cover boards, hinges, and spine.

4. Cut one piece of paper for the inside cover paper that measures 7" x 8" (17.8 cm x 20.3 cm), grain short.

STEP 3:
MAKE THE CASE

1. Place the cover paper facedown on a cutting mat, oriented 8¼" (21 cm) from top to bottom.

2. Draw a vertical line on the cover paper that is 2½" (6.4 cm) from the left edge.

3. Apply glue to the front cover board and center it, with the left edge to the pencil line.

4. Press and rub with waxed paper.

5. Glue on the spine and back cover board, leaving ⅛" (0.3 cm) hinges. Press and rub with waxed paper.

6. Cut and remove a small V of paper at the corner of each cover board, in the ½" (1.3 cm) area toward the top and bottom of the paper, as indicated in the diagram.

Technical note: The inside of the V should align with the edge of the board, and the outside should angle away from the board toward the ends of the paper.

7. Make horizontal scored lines from the corner of each board to the edge of the cover paper (as indicated by the dashed lines in the illustrations).

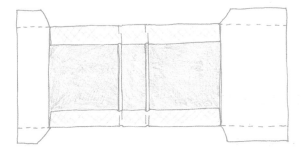

8. Apply glue to the portions of the turn-ins that are above and below the cover and spine boards.

9. Fold the turn-ins over the boards, then press and rub with waxed paper.

Technical note: At this time, do not glue the turn-ins at the ends of the cover paper. (These will be used in the next step to make the pockets.)

10. Glue the inside cover paper, centered head to tail, over the spine and cover boards.

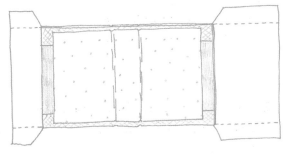

11. Press and rub with waxed paper. Press the inside cover paper slightly into the grooves on both sides of the spine.

Technical note: The inside cover paper does not need to extend from foredge to foredge because the pockets will cover the ends.

STEP 4:
MAKE THE POCKETS

1. Pre-fold the pocket turn-ins along the scored lines.

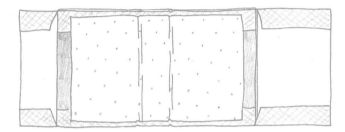

2. Fold the pockets over the board, and crease them tightly against the foredge.

3. Reopen the pockets and the turn-ins, and place the case, with the cover paper faceup, on a piece of scrap paper.

4. Apply glue to the head and tail turn-ins that will be used to make the front pocket.

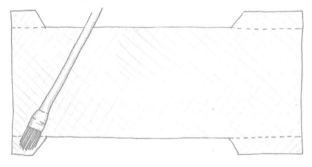

Apply glue to the front side of the cover paper. Do not get glue past the crease or on other parts of the cover paper.

5. Turn the case over so the cover paper is facedown.

6. Fold the turn-ins to create the pocket, press the pocket to the inside of the front cover, and rub with waxed paper.

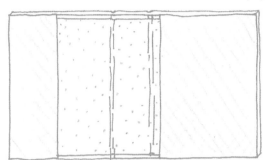

7. Slide a butter knife inside the pocket to make sure it is not stuck shut.

8. Repeat these steps, and glue the back pocket to the back cover.

9. Leave the case to dry under weights.

STEP 5:
ASSEMBLE THE BOOK

1. Slide the stiff back page of the bookblock inside the pocket on the right.

2. Put ephemera, such as photos or paper samples, in the pocket on the left.

RIGHT:

Half Dome from Sentinel Bridge, 1998. 2¾" x 2" (7 cm x 5.1 cm). This book is a variation of the main project. A pamphlet-stitched booklet is attached inside the front pocket and a tunnel book is attached inside the back cover. The tunnel and pamphlet were made using marbled and handmade paper. The book is leather bound with a leather onlay illustration of Half Dome. The title is stamped in gold on the cover.

VARIATIONS

A Papermaking Safari to Africa, 1995. 3" x 2½" (7.6 cm x 6.4 cm). The text is about book and papermaking in South Africa and Zimbabwe, was composed in PageMaker and the initial letters that begin each chapter were illuminated on the linotronic output. Polymer plates were then made and the book was letterpress printed on handmade Zebra Stripe paper, which is white on one side and decorated with zebra stripes made from Zimbabwean plant fibers on the other. The pocket holds samples of paper made in Africa and Zimbabwe and a Zimbabwean $2 bill. 100 copies.

Bayad, 1990. 3½" x 2½" (8.9 cm x 6.4 cm). This book is the story of a trip to the Philippines to discover why there is no history of papermaking in that country. The text was composed in PageMaker, the original copy was illuminated with pen and ink drawings, and the edition was photocopied onto handmade paper (made with Philippine fiber inclusions). Nine separate illustrations were letterpress printed on 3" x 2" (7.6 cm x 5.1 cm) deckled business card blanks that were made in the Philippines from local plant fibers. 50 copies.

We developed the dowel spine portfolio as the binding for a series of miniature broadsides made while we were teaching a workshop at the Naropa Institute's Kavyayantra Press. The press did not have a bindery, so we did not have the usual tools or materials available. That lack was our gain, because it led to the creation of this structure.

The technique is known as non-adhesive binding because no glue is used to hold the structure together. The basic techniques of non-adhesive binding—scoring, folding, and creating flaps or tabs—are used in this project and can also be used to make non-adhesive paper cases for sewn bookblocks or paper-wrapped panels for accordions. Non-adhesive

Wings, 2004. 2¼" x 3" (5.7 cm x 7.6 cm). Peter's stamp collection was used to illustrate a quote by Robinson Jeffers: "Lend me the stone strength of the past and I will lend you the wings of the future, for I have them." Stamps were both glued to the pages and placed in the pockets.

binding creates lightweight, flexible structures, and it requires the use of very few tools or materials. Non-adhesive bindings are not as protective as case bindings, however, and, like origami, the steps are complex to describe in words.

The dowel spine portfolio has proved simple to make while traveling and is a wonderful gift for new acquaintances or valued hosts. We have varied the dimensions of this structure to hold collections of photos, unbound pages of poetry, and printed ephemera. We have even come up with a way to attach pages to the dowel and make a more booklike structure.

The portfolio will measure 4½" x 6⅛" (11.4 cm x 15.5 cm) with a ½" (1.3 cm) spine that is held together by a dowel. The pages are laced over the same dowel.

STEP 1:
PREPARE THE MATERIALS

1. Cut a piece of paper for the cover that measures 11" x 14" (27.9 cm x 35.6 cm), grain short.

2. Cut one to three pieces of paper for pages that measure 4¼" x 12½" (10.8 cm x 31.8 cm), grain short.

3. Cut one length of ¼" (0.6 cm) dowel that measures 4½" (11.4 cm).

STEP 2:
CREATE A ½" (1.3 CM) SPINE IN THE EXACT CENTER OF THE COVER

1. Place the cover paper face down on a cutting mat so that it measures 11" (27.9 cm) from top to bottom.

2. Make marks near each corner that are ½" (1.3 cm) from the edges of the paper.

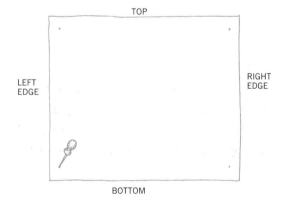

Tip: For accuracy, use an awl. Make the marks by poking a small hole.

Materials

- Paper for cover (medium weight, strong)
- Paper for pages (light to medium weight)
- ¼" (0.6 cm) round wooden dowel (a pencil will also work)

3. Fold the cover paper so the right edge aligns with the holes marked on the left side, then 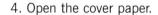 crease.

4. Open the cover paper.

5. Fold the cover paper so the left edge aligns with the holes marked on the right side, and crease the fold.

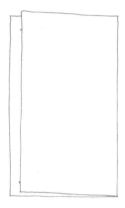

STEP 3:
MARK AND SCORE THE BASIC DIMENSIONS

1. Make a horizontal scored line that is 4" (10.2 cm) from the top. (See "How to Make a Scored Line to Fold Paper," page 18.)

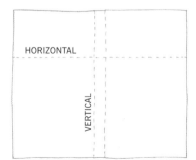

2. Make a second horizontal scored line that is 8½" (21.6 cm) from the top. ●⟁

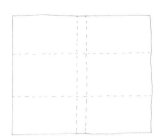

3. Make a vertical scored line that is ½" (1.3 cm) from the left edge. ●⟁

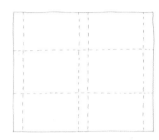

4. Make a second vertical scored line that is ½" (1.3 cm) from the right edge.

STEP 4:
MARK, SCORE, AND CUT THE DIAGONAL POCKET

1. Mark each of the spine folds, 9½" (24.1 cm) from the top. ●⟁

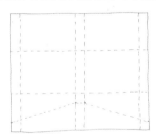

2. Score a line between the marks.

3. Mark both the left and right edges, 10½" (26.7 cm) from the top.

4. Score diagonal lines between the marks on the spine fold and the marks at the edges.

5. Cut off the bottom of the paper ½" (1.3 cm) below these scored lines.

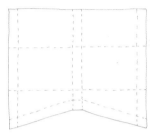

STEP 5:
MAKE THE ANGLE CUTS TO CREATE FLAPS

1. Cut off the bottom left and right corners.

2. Cut and remove a total of six small V-shaped pieces of paper, two at the bottom, two on the left edge, and two on the right edge, all in the ½" (1.3 cm) area between the scored line and the edge of the paper, as indicated in the diagram.

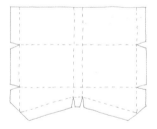

Technical note: These cuts should be about ⅛" to ¼" (0.3 cm to 0.6 cm) wide at the edge of the paper. They will not show when the portfolio is finished. Using a utility knife and a cutting mat, draw the blade from the scored line toward the edge.

STEP 6:
FOLD THE PORTFOLIO

1. Fold the flaps on the left and right edges, then unfold the flap closest to the bottom.

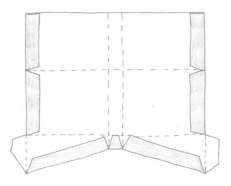

2. Fold the two diagonal flaps and the spine flap.

3. Fold the top down at the horizontal score 4" (10.2 cm) from the top.

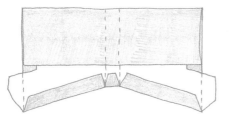

4. Fold the diagonal pocket up at the horizontal score made 8½" (21.6 cm) from the top.

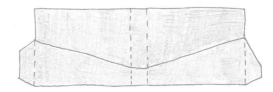

5. Fold and tuck each pocket flap inside the foredge of the portfolio.

Technical note: If desired, these flaps can be sewn, stapled, or glued to secure them in place.

6. Make two slits through the spine, one just above the pocket and the other 1" (2.5 cm) from the head.

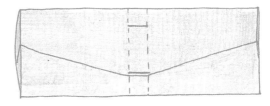

7. To assemble the portfolio, slide the ¼" (0.6 cm) dowel through the spine slits, positioned so that it holds the pocket in place.

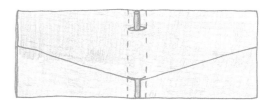

STEP 7:
MAKE THE PAGES

1. Remove the dowel.

2. Place the pages inside the pockets. Make the squares equal on all four sides. The pages may be held in place using binder clips.

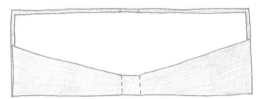

3. Turn the portfolio over.

4. Poke an awl through the ends of each slit to mark the location of the spine in the pages underneath.

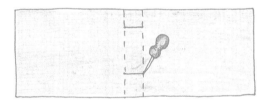

5. Remove the pages from the pockets.

6. One page at a time, use the marks poked in the pages as guides to cut two horizontal slits.

7. Also use the holes to make scored lines from head to tail that indicate the two hinges. Fold the pages along the scored lines.

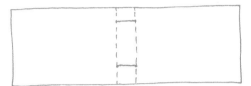

STEP 8:
ATTACH THE PAGES TO THE PORTFOLIO

1. Place the pages inside the portfolio (but not in the pockets).

2. Align the slits and folds.

3. Weave the ¼" (0.6 cm) dowel through the slits in the pages and the portfolio.

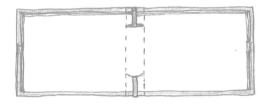

Nine Poets, 1999. 3" x 2½" (7.6 cm x 6.4 cm). Excerpts from poems of nine New York School poets were letterpress printed on small pieces of handmade paper then placed in the pockets of a dowel spine portfolio. The portfolio paper was painted with acrylics for decoration.

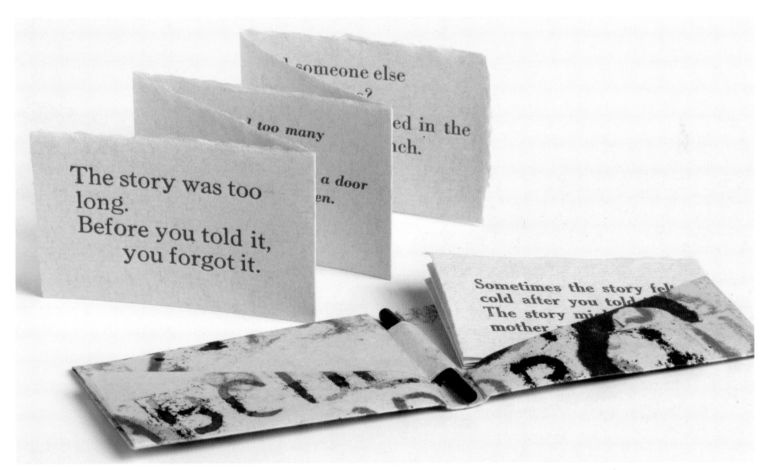

Problems with the Story, 2001. 2½" x 3" (6.4 cm x 7.6 cm). A poem by Naomi Nye was printed on two four-page accordions, and the accordions were then placed in the pockets of a dowel spine portfolio. The cover paper is handmade paper decorated with stenciled pulp paintings.

The idea to make a scroll in a book first came when I was sitting in a history of the book class at the University of Alabama. I had been invited to give a talk to the graduate book arts students and was sampling one of their other classes. In passing, the teacher mentioned that there are certain times in history when things can only be defined by what they are not. In the early twentieth century, a car was called a horseless buggy, a radio was a wireless, and today we call a computer screen a page. This last image, of a scrolling page, inspired me to try and make a book that scrolled like a computer.

We made our first scrolling book, *A 1,000-Mile Walk to the Gulf,* in 1994 (see page 109). It had a wooden scroll bookblock mounted to the back cover. We made more scrolling books and discovered that mounting the bookblock to the spine makes it easier to turn the knob. We also developed several different systems to control the tension on the scroll. The scroll is a wonderful structure, perfect for texts with a burst of monologue, a flowing description, and words or images that an artist would rather not have broken into separate pages. We encourage you to try making other scrolls, both bound and unbound, and explore the possibilities presented by this ancient kind of book.

Love Many Things, 2003.
2¹³⁄₁₆" x 2" (7.1 cm x 5.1 cm). The
hand-painted scroll features
a quote by Vincent van Gogh:
"The best way to know God is
to love many things." The
illustrations feature butterfly
motifs. The case, and the head
and tail of the scroll bookblock
are covered with a paste paper
made by Claire Maziarczyk. The
wood supports are painted with
silver-blue metallic acrylic paint.
An illustration of a butterfly,
painted on paper, is used as a
title on the front cover.

This book will measure 2¹³⁄₁₆" x 2" (7.1 cm x 5.1 cm). It will require a little woodworking. Don't let that intimidate you. If you don't have the tools, ask around your neighborhood. There is usually someone who loves to do little projects like this and will be glad to help you. You can also go to a cabinet shop, where, for a small fee, they will cut wood to the size you require. We recommend using wood with a fine grain that also has a consistent density. Mahogany, maple, or clear pine are all good choices. Balsa wood, although readily available, may not stand up to heavy use.

STEP 1:
CUT THE MATERIALS FOR THE SCROLL STRUCTURE

1. Cut two wood supports that each measure 2½" x ½" x ¼" (6.4 cm x 1.3 cm x 0.6 cm), grain long. ●◗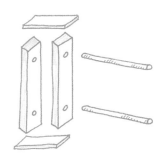

2. Cut a piece of wood that measures 2" x 1¼" x ¾" (5.1 cm x 3.2 cm x 1.9 cm). It will be used to space apart the two wood supports. (The thickness doesn't really matter.)

3. Cut two pieces of ⅛" (0.3 cm) round wooden dowel that each measure 2⅛" (5.4 cm).

4. Cut two pieces of cardboard for the head and tail panels, each measuring 1¾" x ½" (4.4 cm x 1.3 cm), grain long.

Materials

- ½" x ¼" (1.3 cm x 0.6 cm) wood for supports
- ⅛" (0.3 cm) round wood dowel
- Wood for spacer (this can be cut from any wood)
- Cardboard for cover (medium weight)
- Paper for covers (light to medium weight)
- Paper for inside cover paper (light to medium weight)
- Paper for scroll (light weight)

5. Cut two pieces of paper to cover those panels, each measuring 2¾" x 1½" (7 cm x 3.8 cm), grain long.

Technical note: The head and tail panels can be cut from wood, in which case it would not be necessary to cover them.

STEP 2:
DRILL HOLES IN THE WOOD SUPPORTS

1. Make two marks to indicate where to drill the holes on the ½" (1.3 cm) face of one wood support, centered and ⅜" (1 cm) from each end.

2. Clamp the ½" (1.3 cm) faces of the wood supports together. ●◗

3. Drill the holes. Use a drill bit that is slightly larger than the dowel. (Drill a test hole to make sure the dowel will turn in the hole. It is easiest to use a drill press, but a handheld drill will work. Hold it upright and as perpendicular to the wood surface as possible.

STEP 3:
ASSEMBLE THE SCROLL STRUCTURE

1. Cover the head and tail panels. (See "How to Make Panel Covers and Attach an Accordion," step 4, page 46.)

2. Place the two supports on a work surface and place the wood spacer between the wood supports to maintain the proper spacing and keep the supports parallel.

3. Glue the head and tail panels to the wood supports. Use mini bar clamps to clamp the work together.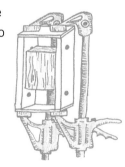

Alternatively, hold it by hand until the glue becomes tacky.

4. Leave to dry for at least an hour.

STEP 4:
MAKE THE CASE

1. Cut two cover boards, each measuring 2¹³⁄₁₆" x 1⅞" (7.1 cm x 4.7 cm), grain long.

2. Cut one spine board that measures 2¹³⁄₁₆" (7.1 cm) tall, grain long. The spine width will be the thickness of the two cover boards plus the thickness of the scroll structure. (See "How to Make a Case and Case-in a Bookblock," step 2, page 51.) The spine for our book measured 2¹³⁄₁₆" x ⅝" (7.1 cm x 1.6 cm), grain long.

3. Cut one piece of paper for the cover that measures 3¾" x 6" (9.5 cm x 15.2 cm), grain short.

4. Cut one piece of paper to line the inside of the case (the inside cover paper) that measures 2⅝" x 4½" (6.7 cm x 11.4 cm). The length will vary depending on the width of the hinges.

5. Glue the spine and cover boards to the cover paper and make the case. (See "How to Make a Case and Case-in a Bookblock," step 5, page 49.)

6. Glue the inside cover paper, centered, on the inside of the case. Press and rub with waxed paper. Press the inside cover paper slightly into the grooves on both sides of the spine.

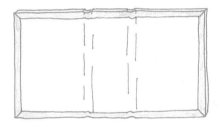

7. Leave the case to dry under weights.

STEP 5:
CASE-IN THE SCROLL STRUCTURE

1. Fold the case around the scroll bookblock, and rub the cover paper flush against the edges of the spine board.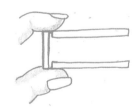

2. Apply glue to the spine end of the scroll structure, and make sure that no glue gets inside the holes.

3. Place the scroll structure, centered, on the spine board.

4. Press and hold it in place until the glue becomes tacky.

5. Let dry for at least an hour.

STEP 6:
ATTACH THE SCROLL

1. Cut one piece of paper for the scroll that measures 14" x 1¼" (35.6 cm x 3.2 cm), grain short.

Technical notes: The scroll can be longer. The scroll is too long if it is fatter than the wood supports when rolled to either end. The width is critical. If the paper is too wide, the scroll will not turn easily.

2. Add text and illustration to the scroll before attaching it. Leave at least 1" (2.5 cm) at each end for gluing.

3. Slide both pieces of ⅛" (0.3 cm) dowel into the holes in the wood supports.

4. Apply glue to the top ½" (1.3 cm) of the side of the scroll paper with text.

5. Wrap the scroll paper around the dowel at the head. Pinch the scroll paper tightly against the dowel.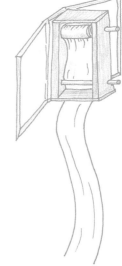

6. Gently roll the scroll onto the dowel.

7. Follow steps 4–6 to glue the bottom of the scroll paper to the dowel at the tail.

8. Leave to dry for at least 10 minutes. If you try to turn the scroll before the glue dries, the paper will not stick to the dowel.

9. After the glue has dried, the scroll can be turned.

Technical notes: Some papers will lay flat and turn easily; others will curl wildly and are difficult to roll on the dowels.

We have made knobs from beads, brass nuts, polymer clay, and paper wrapped around the end of the dowel.

It is best to glue on the knobs with epoxy, because PVA does not always hold.

We have used ⅛" (0.35 cm) brass rod or machine screws in place of wooden dowels.

VARIATIONS

California Dreaming, 2003. 3" x 6" x 3" (7.6 cm x 15.2 cm x 7.6 cm). The lyrics to Jan and Dean's "Surf City" ("I got a '34 wagon and we call it a woodie...") are laser printed on the scroll that also has a hand-painted photo collage of surf and woodie images. The scroll is attached to a brass crank mechanism that is mounted inside a plastic model of a woodie.

A 1,000-Mile Walk to the Gulf, 1994. 2¾" x 2" (7 cm x 5.1 cm). This was our first scrolling book, made in 1994. The text, by John Muir, is letterpress printed with linoleum-cut illustrations. The subject matter of the text is reflected in the choice of materials: knobs of bone; a parchment panel on front; and coarse, natural linen book cloth for the cover.

If It Were Up to Me, 2000. 2" x 3" (5.1 cm x 7.6 cm). The text of this book is a song by Cheryl Wheeler. The bookblock's framework is all wood. The scroll is attached to brass screws that pass through the spine. A system of washers and locking nuts adjusts the tension of the scroll.

Four Views of Kealakekua Bay, 1998. 2¾" x 1¾" (7 cm x 4.4 cm). This book is letterpress printed on handmade paper. There is one pictorial view (a linoleum block illustration cut on site by Donna) and three literary views (one by Captain Cook, one by Mark Twain, and the other is the famous song "Little Grass Shack" by Johnny Noble). The paper was made with two different sides, one white for the image and the other with a pattern that resembles Hawaiian tapa cloth. The wood used is koa, which grows only in Hawaii. The scroll is wrapped around a brass rod, which holds the scroll flat when it is pulled out.

Ulysses, 2000. 13¼" x 7¾" (33.6 cm x 19.7 cm). The pages from a Modern Library edition of James Joyce's *Ulysses* were cut from the book at the spine and glued end to end to make a scroll. As a scroll, the text mimics Joyce's thematic structure: The June day in Dublin and Bloom's life are revealed and left behind, one moment at a time. The scroll is housed in a pine framework painted black, with brass hardware and ebony knobs. A ratcheting device is mounted under the knobs to keep them under tension. The bookblock is mounted into a full leather case with the original book covers affixed as decorative panels. Mirrors on the inside of the covers reflect images of the scrolled text.

Pandora's Box, 1997. 1" x 2¼" (2.5 cm x 5.7 cm). I read *Slaughterhouse Five* by Kurt Vonnegut and found this quote buried in the middle of the book. It struck me that his words were like the hope left in the bottom of Pandora's Box, and that inspired the idea to make the book a scroll in a box. The text is letterpress printed from metal type and linoleum blocks. The box is made with wooden end panels and handmade knobs. We marbled the cover paper, and the title is stamped in gold on the front panel.

The invention of our scrolling book led to a period of exploration. We began to try to find the limits of what a book could be. We became intrigued by the idea of making a book that had all the elements of a traditional book but each in unexpected locations. Could we put the text on the cover? Could the decorative cover somehow be on the inside? These ideas led to sketches and models.

One result was the binding for the special copies of *Meditations at the Edge* (see page 119). The text discusses how paper has been used to connect the spiritual and the physical worlds in the East, and meditates on how this contrasts with practices in the West. We wanted a

binding that merged Eastern and Western traditions, and we began to think of the pages as prayer flags. Memories of work by Helmut Becker, a paper artist from Canada (handmade paper draped over sticks), led us to imagine a book in which the pages were actual flags. We glued each printed page to a wooden dowel and mounted them in a beautiful wooden framework as a binding. Further exploration on this theme led to the creation of the doweled flap book described in this project. Early versions had the flap bookblock mounted to the spine. Influenced by the concept of the book as a container in which openings and closings hide and reveal images, we began to attach the bookblock to the inside of the back cover. In this way, an image or message is revealed whenever the horizontal flaps are raised.

Baby Suzanne, 2003. 2⅞" x 1⅞" (7.3 cm x 4.7 cm). We made this book to celebrate the birth of our second daughter. The cover is a cotton print fabric. The illustrations are hand-colored photocopies of photographs. The flap bookblock is made with wood that has been painted with acrylic paint. The flaps are handmade paper. When the flaps are turned horizontal, an image of the new baby can be seen.

This book will measure 2⅞" x 1⅞" (7.3 cm x 4.8 cm). Techniques and ideas used to make the scrolling book (see page 104) are also used in this project. An image or message can be placed on the inside cover paper, under the flap bookblock, which will be revealed when the flaps are horizontal. The book we made for this project is covered with cloth, but it can also be covered in paper, and the instructions will refer to using paper.

STEP 1:
MAKE THE FLAP BOOKBLOCK

1. Cut five 2⅛" (5.4 cm) lengths of ⅛" (0.3 cm) wooden dowel. These will be used to turn the flaps.

2. Cut two pieces of cardboard for the head and tail panels, each measuring 1¾" x ½" (4.4 cm x 1.3 cm), grain long.

3. Cut two pieces of paper to cover those panels each measuring 2¾" x 1½" (7 cm x 3.8 cm), grain long.

4. Cut five pieces of paper for the flaps, each measuring 1¾" x 1³⁄₁₆" (4.4 cm x 3 cm), grain short.

5. Mark the location of the five holes on one of the wood supports. Make all marks centered on the ½" (1.3 cm) face of the support: Make the first mark ¼" (0.6 cm) from the head. Make the four marks below that, ⅜" (1 cm) apart. (The spaces are not even at the head and tail for a reason: Because all the flaps are the same size, this creates equal visual spacing when the flaps are all down.)

Materials

- ½" x ¼" (1.3 cm x 0.6 cm) wood for supports
- ⅛" (0.3 cm) round wooden dowel
- 2" x 1¼" x ½" (5.1 cm x 3.2 cm x 1.3 cm) wood spacer
- Paper for flaps (light to medium weight)
- Cardboard for panel (light to medium weight)
- Paper for panel cover (light to medium weight)
- Cardboard for cover (medium weight)
- Paper for cover and inside cover (light to medium weight)

6. Clamp the ½" (1.3 cm) faces of the wood supports together. Using a drill bit that is slightly larger than the ⅛" (0.3 cm) round dowel (³⁄₁₆" or ⁵⁄₃₂" [4.8 mm or 4 mm]), drill the holes.

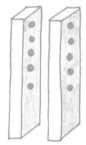

We usually use a drill press to make the holes, but a handheld drill will work. Hold it upright and as perpendicular to the wood surface as possible. We do not drill all the way through the bottom board, but it will not matter if you drill all the way through. (We leave ¹⁄₃₂" to ¹⁄₁₆" [0.75 mm to 1.6 mm].)

Make the panels for the head and tail of the flap bookblock. (See "How to Make Panel Covers and Attach an Accordion," step 4, page 46.) These head and tail panels can also be cut from wood and left uncovered. ●◆

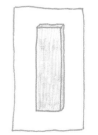

7. Place the two wooden supports on a work surface, with the holes properly oriented. Place the wood spacer between the wood supports (to maintain the proper spacing and to keep the supports parallel).

8. Glue the head and tail panels to the wood supports. ●◆

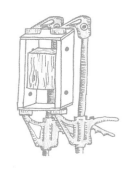

Use mini bar clamps to hold it together while drying. Alternatively, hold it until the glue adheres. ●◆

9. Let dry for at least an hour.

10. After it is completely dry, paint the flap bookblock structure and the dowels.

STEP 2:
ATTACH THE FLAP PAGES

1. Fold the flap pages in half, oriented so that they are 1³⁄₁₆" (3 cm) wide.

2. To add illustration or text, refer to the diagram to orient the text correctly. ●◆

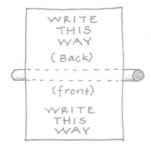

3. Insert a dowel into the holes at the head of the flap bookblock.

4. Apply glue to the undecorated side of the first flap.

5. Insert the flap from the back of the flap block, and slip it over the dowel. ●◆

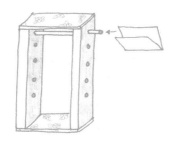

Make sure the text is oriented correctly. Align the two foredges, press the flap together, and pinch the paper tightly where it meets after circling the dowel.

6. Turn the flap so that it rests against the head of the bookblock. ●◆

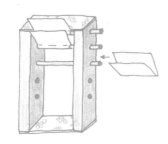

7. Follow steps 4–6 to glue the other four flaps in place.

STEP 3:

MAKE THE PANEL TO BE GLUED INSIDE THE FRONT COVER

1. Cut cardboard for the panel that measures 2⅝" x 1¾" (6.7 cm x 4.4 cm), grain long.

2. Cut paper for the panel cover paper that measures 3⅝" x 2¾" (9.2 cm x 7 cm), grain long.

3. Make the panel. (See "How to Make Panel Covers and Attach an Accordion," step 4, page 46.)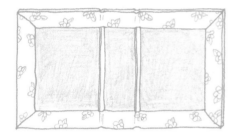

STEP 4:

MAKE THE CASE

1. Cut two cover boards, each measuring 2 1³⁄₁₆" x 1⅞" (7.1 cm x 4.7 cm), grain long.

2. Cut the spine board that measures 2 1³⁄₁₆" (7.1 cm) high, grain long. The spine width will be the thickness of two cover boards, plus one panel board, plus the thickness of the flap bookblock. (See "How to Make a Case and Case-in a Bookblock," step 2, page 49.) The spine board for our book measured 2 1³⁄₁₆" x 1¹⁄₁₆" (7.1 cm x 1.7 cm), grain long.

3. Cut paper for the cover that measures 3¾" x 6" (9.5 cm x 15.2 cm), grain short.

4. Cut paper to cover the inside of the case (the inside cover paper) that measures 2 ⅝" x 4⅜" (6.7 cm x 11.2 cm), grain short.

Technical note: Keep the following details in mind regarding the inside cover paper:

■ It will be covered on the left by the panel.

■ It will show at the spine.

■ It will be covered by the flap bookblock on the right, but it will show when the flaps are turned horizontally.

■ If you plan to have an image or text that will show when the flaps are turned horizontally, it must be added before the flap bookblock is glued in place.

5. Make the case. (See "How to Make a Case and Case-in a Bookblock," step 5, page 49.)

6. Glue the inside cover paper, centered, on the inside of the case.

7. Press and rub with waxed paper. Press the inside cover paper slightly into the grooves on both sides of the spine.

8. Glue the panel, centered, on the inside of the front cover. ●◆

9. Press and place under weight to dry.

STEP 5:
ASSEMBLE THE BOOK

1. Fold the case around the flap bookblock and flatten the hinge paper to the edges of the spine by rubbing with a bone folder. (See "How to Make a Case and Case-in a Bookblock," step 6, page 51.)

2. Glue the flap bookblock to the inside of the back cover. ●◆

Leave 1/16" (1.6 mm) squares at the head, tail, and foredge. The bookblock should rest against the spine when the book is closed.

3. Leave under weights to dry.

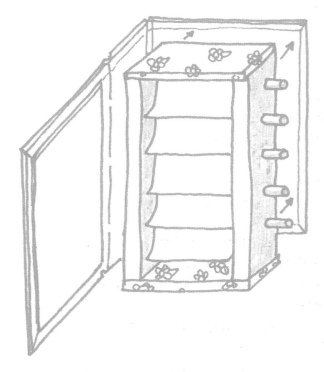

Time I$, 2003. 2⅞" x 2" (7.3 cm x 5.1 cm). This is the first time we created a hiding place by mounting the flap bookblock to the back cover. The front side of the flap is what Ben Franklin had to say about time and money; what Mark Twain had to say is on the back. What Peter had to say is on the cover, endpages, and the American $1 bill, which can be removed from behind the text. The book was letterpress printed on handmade paper, using old wood and metal types and images of clocks carved out of linoleum. The cover and endpages both required at least 10 press runs to print all the different clocks and the various settings of "time is time." The $1 bills were ordered direct from the U.S. Treasury and are sequentially numbered, thus the number on the bill matches the book's edition number. 100 copies.

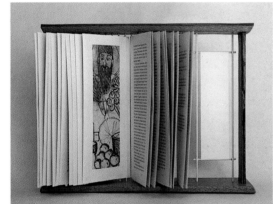

Meditations at the Edge, 1996. 12½" x 16" x 3⅞" (31.8 cm x 40.6 cm x 9.8 cm). Text by Dorothy Fields. One of fourteen special copies.

Forty, 1997. 2¾" x 2" (7 cm x 5.1 cm). This is the first book we made using this structure. The quote, "Art is long, life is short," was letterpress printed on handmade paper, with 15 colored press runs using various representations of the number forty. The book is paper bound using the same handmade paper. 40 copies.

The dowel spine binding may be one of the most complex structures we have developed, but it began as a simple challenge. We had made a number of different books using a dowel as a major structural element of the binding. Many people expressed interest in these books. We began to notice that other artists were also making books that used dowels or wooden skewers. We joked that the accordion had seen its 15 minutes of fame and the next bookbinding fad would be books made with dowels. With some further thought we gave the genre a name: stick structures.

During this same time, Donna had taken a cross-country ski trip in Yosemite and had gone up Mt. Dana. Near the top, as she watched crows circling overhead, she was inspired to cut the blocks for a book to be titled *The View from Mt. Dana* (see opposite page). I challenged her to design a new stick structure binding for the book. The result was the combination of a piano hinge with an accordion book, with the accordion also acting as the spine, which she called the dowel hinge spine accordion book.

The View from Mt. Dana, 1997. 2¾" x 2³⁄₁₆" (7 cm x 5.6 cm). When skiing in the Sierra Nevada mountains, Donna climbed Mt. Dana, saw the vast panorama with the crows soaring, and thought of a quote by John Muir: "As we go on and on studying this old, old life in the light of the life beating warmly about us, we enrich and lengthen our own." Based on sketches made during that trip, Donna took up her tools and cut the lettering and the illustration, at this miniature size, into three sets of linoleum blocks. The text was letterpress printed from the linoleum-cut blocks, in three colors, on handmade paper. 97 copies. Three copies of the edition have a special binding made with blue Moroccan goat leather. A silver-paper inlayed line on the cover defines a gray leather panel that has a crow onlay. Silver rods replace dowels at the hinge.

This book will measure 2¾" x 2³⁄₁₆" (7 cm x 5.6 cm). The accordion bookblock is a single sheet of paper that has an eight-page accordion (the pages each measure 2⅝" x 1⅞" [6.7 cm x 4.7 cm]), two endpages, and a slit spine.

Materials

- Paper for the accordion bookblock (medium weight)
- Cardboard for the covers (medium weight)
- Paper for the covers (medium weight)
- ⅛" (0.3 cm) round wooden dowel

STEP 1:
PREPARE THE ACCORDION

1. Cut a piece of paper that measures 2⅝" x 19½" (6.7 cm x 49.5 cm), grain short.

2. Measure and draw a line that is 1⅞" (4.8 cm) from the left edge of the accordion paper. This will indicate the position of the left endpage.

3. Draw a second line 2⅝" (6.7 cm) from the left edge (¾" [1.9 cm] to the right of the first line). This will indicate the position of the spine.

4. Mark and cut six horizontal slits in the spine. Position these slits ¼", ⅝", and 1⅛" (0.6 cm, 1.6 cm, and 2.8 cm) from both the head and the tail of the accordion paper.

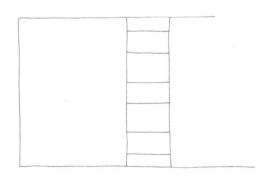

5. Make a scored line that is 4½" (11.4 cm) from the left edge (1⅞" [4.7 cm] from the second pencil line). This will indicate the position of the right endpage.

6. Fold the right edge of the accordion paper to the line just scored, and continue folding to make an eight-page accordion. (See "How to Fold an Accordion," page 24.) Each page will measure 2⅝" x 1⅞" (6.7 cm x 4.7 cm).

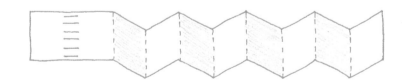

STEP 2:
PREPARE THE COVER MATERIALS

1. Cut two cover boards, each measuring 2¾" x 1¹⁵⁄₁₆" (7 cm x 4.9 cm), grain long. ¹⁄₁₆" *(1.6 mm) squares*

2. Cut two pieces of paper to cover the boards, each measuring 3½" x 3¼" (8.9 cm x 8.2 cm), grain long.

3. Cut two pieces of paper for the inside of the covers (inside cover papers), each measuring 2⅝" x 1 1³⁄₁₆" (6.7 cm x 4.6 cm), grain long.

4. Cut three pieces of ⅛" (0.3 cm) dowel, each measuring 2¾" (7 cm) long.

5. Cut one piece of ⅛" (0.3 cm) dowel that is 6" (15.2 cm) long. Sand or carve a point on one end to make a skewer.

STEP 3:
MAKE THE COVERS WITH LOOPED FLAP HINGES

1. Place one cover paper facedown, measuring 3½" (8.9 cm) from head to tail.

2. Draw a vertical line on the cover paper that is ⅜" (1 cm) from the left edge. Apply glue to one of the cover boards and place it, centered, with the left edge to the line. Press and rub with waxed paper. ●◗

3. Apply glue to the turn-ins at the head, tail, and foredge. ●◗

4. Miter the corners at the foredge. Do not miter turn-ins at the spine, just fold them over and press them in place to create a hinge flap. Rub with waxed paper. ●◗

5. Orient the cover with the hinge flap to the right and the folded-over turn-ins facing up.

6. Place the left endpage of the accordion on top of the cover.

Make sure the squares at the head, tail, and foredge are all equal. When positioned correctly, the left ends of the slits will all be aligned with the cover board's edge.

7. Use the accordion paper as a template to mark the location of the spine slits on the hinge flap by poking an awl through the left end of each slit.

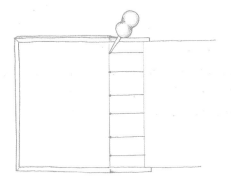

8. Using a triangle ruler as a guide, draw pencil lines perpendicular to the cover board, marking the location of the slits on the hinge flap. ●◆

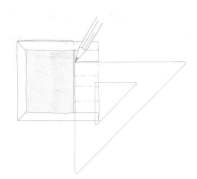

Use a sharp utility knife to cut slits along those lines, creating seven separate flaps. It is important that these slits are cut perpendicular to the cover board. ●◆

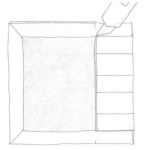

Apply glue to the second, fourth, and sixth flaps, fold them over the edge of the cover board, and press them to the inside of the cover. Rub with waxed paper. ●◆

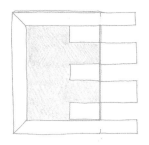

9. Mark a line from head to tail on the unfolded flaps that is 7/16" (11.2 cm) from the edge of the cover board. ●◆

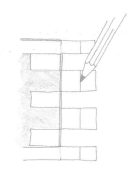

10. Apply glue to the flaps, from that line toward the ends of the flaps. ●◆

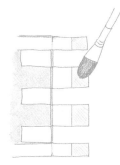

11. Place a dowel along the right edge of the cover board. Wrap the flaps around the dowel. Press the flaps to the inside of the cover board. This will create four looped flaps that circle the dowel. Press and rub with waxed paper. ●◆

12. Remove the dowel.

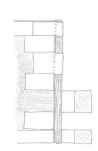

13. Glue the inside panel cover paper, centered, on the cover board. Press and rub with waxed paper. ●◆

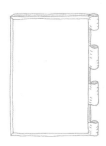

14. Leave under weight to dry.

15. Repeat steps 1–14 to make the other cover.

STEP 4:
ASSEMBLE THE BOOK

1. Place the front cover face down, with the hinge to the right. Then place the accordion paper's left endpage on top of the front cover. The spine slits should align with the loops.

2. Slide the skewer through the loops and weave it through alternate spine slits in the accordion paper (at the left end of the slits).

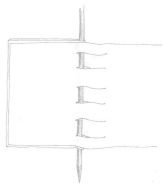

3. Use a 2¾" (7 cm) dowel to push the skewer out of the hinge, carefully sliding the dowel in place as the skewer is forced out. Place the back cover facedown, with the hinges facing left, under the right endpage of the accordion paper. The spine slits should align with the loops.

4. Slide the skewer through the loops, and weave it through alternate spine slits in the accordion paper (at the right end of the slits).

5. Replace the skewer with a 2¾" (7 cm) dowel.

6. Weave the skewer through alternating spine slits in the accordion (between the two dowels). This will lace the spine together.

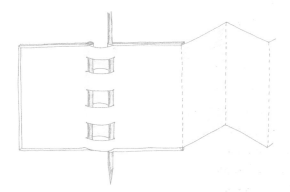

7. Replace the skewer with a 2¾" (7 cm) dowel.

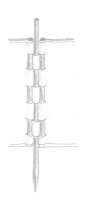

8. The binding is now complete and the accordion can be folded and placed inside the covers.

Sit and Knit, 2004. 4⅜" x 3⅜" (11.2 cm x 8.6 cm). Small knitted panels and a text by William Howitt written in 1844 describing rural knitters in England in the nineteenth century are sewn to the accordion pages of a dowel hinge spine accordion book. The text reads, "…the whole troop of neighbors being collected, they sit and knit, sing knitting songs and tell knitting stories." Instead of dowels, the spine is made with knitting needles. The handmade paper is decorated with acrylic paint and crayon.

An Historical View of Shoes and a Quote from Hamlet, 2003. 1⅞" x 2¼" (4.7 cm x 5.7 cm). In this book, two more layers of accordions are added to a standard dowel hinge spine accordion binding, creating a triple layer, six-page accordion. The outer accordions have been cut with shoe shapes, painted, and finished with written text. A title panel is sewn onto the free endpage. Peter made the paper for the accordions, and Peggy Skycraft marbled the paper for the covers.

Alphabet Pulp, 2001. 2¾" x 2³⁄₁₆" (7 cm x 5.6 cm). Peter made paper using alphabet stencils to create pulp-painted decorations. This paper was used to make the covers of this book as well as the panels that have been sewn to the accordion pages.

Sculpture is three-dimensional, and it can be grasped in one viewing. The artist's book is four-dimensional—it has the fourth dimension of time; time is required to view the complete work, to turn the pages, and to see the sequence of the text. As we began to think of the book as a literary object rather than a literary vehicle, we began to make books from found objects.

In books made out of objects, the object usually inspires the content. For example, we made two books, *The Real Accordion Book* (see page 132) and *The Real Concertina Binding*, (see page 133) from real instruments. The text of *The Real Accordion Book* is visual, autobiographical, and instructional. The text of *The Real Concertina Binding* is a collection of limericks about the concertina. The real purpose of making the two books was to playfully address a point of confusion among book artists: whether a folded paper book should be called an accordion or a concertina. I had played both musical instruments, so I knew that an accordion is rectangular and a concertina is hexagonal. These books were made to present graphically the idea that the only correct term is accordion, unless a book is hexagonal in shape, in which case it is then correct to call it a concertina! Every three-dimensional object has potential sites for pages and the potential to become an artist's book. Pages can be glued to the surface. If an object can be opened, it can act as a case; if not, it can act as a panel cover. Most objects can be sliced in half to create front and back covers for a bookblock. If the object has caverns, they can be used to house a scroll. The possibilities are unlimited.

Rather than presenting instructions for a specific project, we will feature five examples. Once you decide on a found object, you can use a number of the book structures you've already learned to create a found object book.

This project will use old cameras to give five examples of how an object can be used to make a book. Rather than giving specific measurements for materials (because they will vary depending on your specific object), we tell you how we determined the measurements for the project, so that it may provide a guideline for determining the measurements for yours.

EXAMPLE 1: ●◖◗
THE CAMERA AS A PANEL COVER WITH A SEWN BOOKBLOCK

1. Cut the camera in half using a fine tooth hacksaw.

2. Take measurements and make panel covers slightly larger than the camera halves.

3. Glue the panel covers to each half of the camera using silicone adhesive.

4. Measure and cut pages to make a bookblock that will leave $\frac{1}{16}$" (1.6 mm) squares when cased-in.

5. Sew the textblock. (See "How to Sew Multiple Sections for a Miniature Textblock," page 34.)

6. Glue the endpages to the panel covers to complete the binding.

Australian Birds, 2004. 3" x 5" x 2" (7.6 cm x 12.7 cm x 5.1 cm). An Ultronic Panoramic camera was used to make this book about birds that we wish we had taken pictures of when we were in Australia. Collaged images and text from a book about Australian birds have been glued to the pages of a blank book made with handmade paper. The camera was first sawed in half using a hacksaw. Measurements were taken and text was created to fit between th halves. The text was sewn, panel covers were glued to each endpage, and the camera halves were glued to the outside of the covers.

EXAMPLE 2: ●◆
THE CAMERA DOORS AS A CASE
(WITH ACCORDION PAGES)

1. Use the camera doors like the case of a case binding.

2. Saw and sand the surfaces flat.

3. Take measurements to determine the maximum page size.

4. Make an accordion textblock, and glue it into the front and back covers.

Waves of Santa Cruz, 2004. 2½" x 5" x 1¾" (6.4 cm x 12.7 cm x 4.4 cm). A Vivitar EZ35 camera was used to make this book, which features pictures taken in Santa Cruz. Often in panoramic ocean scenes, waves end up as little lines across the print. By using the long narrow landscape format, we could cut up our old photos and properly present the scenes of waves and surf. The cut-up photographs have been glued to accordion pages made from handmade paper.

EXAMPLE 3: ●◆
THE CAMERA DOORS AS A CASE
(WITH AN ACCORDION PLEAT SPINE
BOOKBLOCK).

1. Use the bellow cavity to hold the pages and the camera's door as the back cover.

2. Measure and make a panel cover that will fit in the bellow cavity.

3. Make an accordion pleat spine and glue images to the spine.

4. Attach endpages to the pleat spine, and then glue them to the panel covers.

5. Glue the front panel cover into the bellow cavity, and glue the back panel cover to the camera's door.

Mary Jane 1907–2001, 2004. 3½" x 5¼" x 2¾" (8.9 cm x 13.3 cm x 7 cm). Our Grandma Mary's old Beacon 225 camera was used to make this book. It features pictures from one of her old photo albums. The photos (which may have been taken with that very camera) were color copied and cut to size, then glued to the accordion pleat spine. Lace from Grandma Mary's sewing basket was attached behind the accordion in the old path of the film.

EXAMPLE 4: ●◆
THE CAMERA WITH SCROLLING TEXT.

1. Use a scrolling text to mimic the path of the film.

2. Drill holes through the camera body at the center of the film rolling mechanisms, and remove all the mechanisms.

3. Slide a ⅛" (0.25 cm) brass rod, bent with a crank at the end, into the holes.

Technical note: You can use a wooden dowel in place of the brass rod.

4. Take measurements. Cut and illustrate the scroll paper.

5. Glue the scroll paper to the brass cranks.

A Surfing Safari, 2004. 2½" x 4½" x 1¾" (6.4 cm x 11.4 cm x 4.4 cm). An Ansco Pix Panoramic camera was used to make this scrolling camera book. The scroll is a hand-colored, laser-printed collage of panoramic images taken at San Onofre, a surfing beach in southern California.

EXAMPLE 5: ●◆
THE BELLOWS AS A BOX FOR A BOOK

1. Use the bellows like a hollow book, or a box.

2. Take measurements.

3. Make an accordion textblock, and place it into the cavity.

Flashback, 2004. 2½" x 5" x 1¾" (6.4 cm x 12.7 cm x 4.4 cm). Peter's old Kodak Instamatic 104 camera was used to make this book. Photographs taken between 1969 and 1974 were color copied. The copies were cut up and glued to pages of an accordion bookblock with foldouts. The accordion was made using handmade paper.

The Real Accordion Book, 2001. 16" x 16" x 6" (40.6 cm x 40.6 cm x 15.2 cm). This book uses a vintage two-row bass piano accordion to make a "real" accordion book. Peter bought the accordion at the San Luis Obispo flea market in 1977, intending to learn to play it. He never really learned to play this instrument, but he did learn to play the button accordion. (We have not made any books out of button accordions.) The bellows were cut so that they would fold as an accordion book. The keyboard and button boxes were attached as covers. The book is about setting the record straight and the artistic struggle to master one's craft. It features manipulated found images, laser printed on handmade paper and hand colored.

The Real Concertina Binding, 2001.
7" x 7" x 7" (17.8 cm x 17.8 cm x 17.8 cm).
This book uses a very cheap concertina to make a "real" concertina book. Peter's dad bought the concertina in England, intending to learn to play it. He never learned to play the instrument, and he gave it to Peter, who didn't even try to play it. The bellows were cut to form an accordion pleat spine, and the pages were sewn between the pleats. The two button boxes were attached as covers. The text is a collection of limericks that feature the concertina. It was hand lettered and painted on handmade paper.

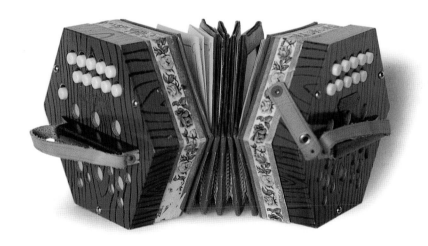

For years we have made hollowed books to sell at crafts fairs as boxes—places to hide gum or candy when in class or to hide a small whiskey bottle when in church. There is a moral dilemma when hollowing out (or altering) a book: Is something of great value being ruined? If it was found at a library used book sale, then it probably is not valuable, but it is always a good idea to check with a knowledgeable bookseller.

Books are often used in artwork. As a genre, these books are known as "altered books." In some altered books, we work with the pages, painting them, changing the text, and adding collaged images. For others, we add objects and ephemera to the covers or inside the book to create dioramas or shrines. Because many of these artworks lack movement (i.e., turning of pages) and other booklike qualities, for many people it is hard to understand why such objects are called books instead of sculpture. And it was like that for us, too, until we made one.

Between 1996 and 2003, we made a group of artists' books that we called the Ukulele Book Series (see page 138). These twenty-five book objects attempt to represent, or depict, every kind of book structure, or book concept, using a ukulele as part of the book. Because we also make hollow books, one piece in the series is a ukulele made from a hollowed book. And, because book artists use cigar boxes (with objects or ephemera inside) to make artists' books, and instrument makers use cigar boxes to make ukuleles, another book in the series is a cigar box ukulele with a diorama inside. Creating the cigar box–ukulele book was so fun that we actually made two, and in the process we came to understand why a diorama is a book: because it tells a story. The story may be as obtuse as abstract poetry or as evident as prose, and it may be different for each viewer. At times, dioramas take on a life of their own, and the story is not the one the artist had in mind. This project will describe one way to make an altered book. We will reveal our "secret patented method" for making hollow books. The rest will be up to you.

Wheel World, 2004. 6¾" x 4³⁄₁₆" (17.1 cm x 10.6 cm). This paperback copy of *Wheel World* was hollowed out and painted with acrylic paints. The hole in the book displays a collection of slot car wheels Peter has been saving since he raced slot cars in his elementary school days.

The instructions for this project will describe making a hollowed book with a few pages left at the front and a hole drilled all the way through the center of the bookblock, but not through the back cover.

Note: Although it is not an infringement of copyright laws to use purchased items, including books, in your artwork, it may be a copyright infringement to reproduce images of that artwork.

STEP 1:
PLAN THE HOLE

1. Decide which size hole will be made and where it will be located. Keep in mind that:

- the hole can go all the way through the book and the covers,

- the hole can use the back cover as its bottom,

- the hole can be split in half so that there are hollow spaces on both sides of the open book, and

- more than one hole can be made.

STEP 2:
DRILL THE HOLE

1. Cut one piece of Masonite and one piece of plywood, each measuring approximately the same size as the book.

2. Place the piece of plywood behind the last page to be drilled through.

3. Place the Masonite in front of the first page to be drilled through.

Materials

- Hardbound book
- Found objects
- ⅛"-thick (0.3 cm) Masonite or cardboard
- ½" to ¾" (1.3 cm to 1.9 cm) thick plywood or pressed wood board
- Electric drill
- Hole saw bit attachments for an electric drill

4. Make sure the bookblock is square and clamp the pages tightly, between the cardboard and plywood, using a bar clamp at each corner.

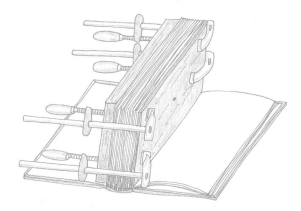

5. Mark the center of the hole to be drilled on the Masonite.

6. Set up the hole saw so that the bit extends about ¾" (1.9 cm) try to avoid breaching conversion beyond the edge of the hole saw blade.

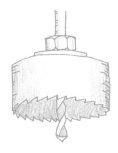

7. Insert the hole saw into the drill.

8. Line up the bit at the center of the hole, saw to the mark, and drill through the Masonite.

Technical notes: Keep the drill perpendicular to the book. Allow the drill to obtain maximum speed, and then ease it into the book. Let the hole saw's blade do the cutting. Do not force it, or the pages of the book may tear. There will be lots of dust, so wear a dust mask.

9. When the drill has cut through the Masonite, stop drilling. Pull the Masonite and any pages that have been cut free out of the cavity in the hole saw.

Technical notes: Keep the drill turning as you pull it out of the hole.

Use a heavy-duty awl to help pry the Masonite and drilled pages out of the cavity in the hole saw.

10. Continue drilling until the hole saw cuts into the plywood backing and all the pages have been cut out.

Technical note: The pages may fill up the cavity of the hole saw several times before the hole is complete.

11. Cut additional holes if desired.

STEP 3:
GLUE THE HOLE TOGETHER

1. Remove the clamps, cardboard, and plywood.

2. Clear out any paper dust or torn paper.

3. Apply glue to the edges of the cut hole. Spread some glue around the bottom of the hole so it will adhere to the back cover.

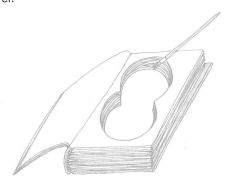

4. Place waxed paper over the hole, and close the book.

5. If the book has a spine that will be crushed when pressing, place a piece of cardboard over the front and back covers, leaving the hinge and spine exposed.

6. Press the book under weight. Make sure there is enough pressure to keep the pages from warping around the hole as the glue dries.

STEP 4:
DECORATE THE BOOK AS DESIRED

Mystic Isles of the South Seas (the Real Fake Uke), 2000. 18" x 6" x 2¾" (45.7 cm x 15.2 cm x 7 cm). The neck of a ukulele was attached through the top end of a copy of *Mystic Isles of the South Seas* by Fredrick O'Brien. A sound hole was drilled through the cover, revealing some of the text, and a bridge was mounted on the cover below the sound hole. The book opens at the back cover; the title page was moved to the back of the book so it could still be read.

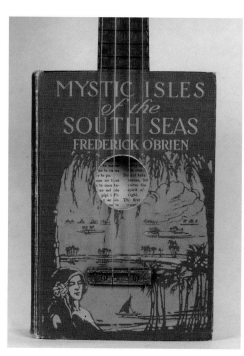

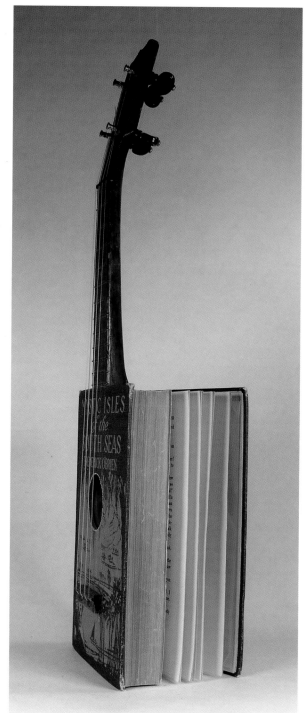

Our Young Folks Jeff Grell, 2003. 7¾" x 5⅜" (19.7 cm x 13.7 cm). A copy of *Our Young Folks Plutarch* (1883) was hollowed out and painted with acrylic paints by Suzanne Thomas. A scroll, connected to a brass crank, was then mounted in the hole. The text is a short biography of Grell, the first person to attach a high back binding to a snowboard. It is inkjet printed on handmade paper. The small bottle below the scroll symbolizes Grell's passion for collecting old bottles.

Man and Wave, 1999. 8" x 5⅝" (20.3 cm x 14.3 cm). This altered book was made by Suzanne Thomas. Collage is used over the text. The hollow center is designed as a surfer's shrine filled with shells.

The "History of the Ukulele" Cigar Box Ukulele, 2002. 16" x 6" x 3" (40.6 cm x 15.2 cm x 7.6 cm). A cigar box was attached to a ukulele neck. Inside the cigar box is a diorama that tells a story about the history of the ukulele and the allure of the tropical paradise where it originated. Our miniature book *A Brief History of the Ukulele* is mounted on a hinged wooden flap.

Glossary

Accordion fold: a single sheet of paper folded back and forth

Accordion pleat: a tall, narrow accordion fold

Adhesive: substance used to adhere (e.g., glue, paste, glue stick, epoxy)

Archival: material that has the ability to stay stable over time

Back: the side of the book following the bookblock

Basis weight: the weight of a ream (500 sheets) of paper at the parent sheet size

Board: the cardboard used for covers, spines, and cases.

Bone folder: a piece of bone used to smooth folds and create score lines

Bookblock: the textblock, ready for binding, with endpages in place.

Burnish: to make a surface shiny by rubbing

Case: the cover of a book, made separate from the bookblock

Clamshell: a protective box for a book, which opens like a book

Codex: a book in which the pages are attached at the spine

Cover: the outside protection for a book, usually cardboard wrapped with paper, cloth, or leather

Cover board: the cardboard used to make a cover or case

Cover material: the paper, cloth, or leather used for a cover

Deckle: the feathered edge on a piece of paper, created during the papermaking process

Diorama: three-dimensional miniature scene in which objects are arranged against a painted background

Endpage: the paper preceding and following the textblock

Face: the outside surface of the book

Facedown: the outside, decorated side, or "right" side of the material facing away from you or toward the work surface

Faceup: the outside, decorated side, or "right" side of the material facing toward you

Fine press: the printing aesthetic that pays particular attention to typography; the printing process used is usually letterpress

Folio: a single sheet of paper, folded in half to create four pages

Foredge: the front edge of a book

Front: the side of the book preceding the bookblock

Glue: the process of adhering; also the word used for PVA

Head: the top of the book

Headbands: the decorative stitching on the head and tail of the bookblock that is either hand stitched or purchased in a premade ribbon

Hinge: the joint between the front (or back) cover and the spine

Inside cover paper: paper glued to the inside of a case or panel cover

Leaf: a single sheet of paper

Leather onlay: very thin leather pasted to the cover of a book

Margin: the space near the foredge, head, or tail of a printed page

Mountain fold: the fold of an accordion that has the peak pointing up

Non-adhesive binding: a binding that is made without using adhesive

Panel cover: a board wrapped on all four sides

Parent sheet: A sheet of paper that is the size it was made (or originally cut from the roll); this size differs from grade to grade

Paste: an adhesive used for its archival quality and reversibility, usually starch based

Ply: the layers of a laminated piece of paper or cardboard

Recto: the front side of a piece of paper, usually the odd-numbered pages

Ream: a prepackaged stack of paper, usually 500 sheets

Reversible: the quality of an adhesive that allows it to be removed without damage to the previously adhered surfaces

Score: a depressed line that is commonly made with a bone folder

Section: an assembled group of pages (usually folded) that form part of a textblock

Sewing station: locations marked on a section that are used to indicate where to sew

Slipcase: a protective box that is open on one end

Spine: the back edge of the book that is sewn; also the part of the binding that covers it

Spine lining: material glued over the spine of a bookblock as reinforcement

Square: the area of the cover that extends beyond the bookblock

Super: material used for the spine lining, usually loose-weave cotton

Tail: the bottom edge of a book

Textblock: the assembled pages of a book without endpages

Tip in: the process of attaching a smaller page, adhered along one edge, to another page

Turn-in: the edge of the cover material that wraps around the edge of the board, past the square, and underneath the endpage

Valley fold: the fold of an accordion that has the valley pointing down

Verso: the back of a piece of paper, usually the even-numbered pages

RESOURCES

AUSTRALIA

Artwise Amazing Paper
186 Enmore Rd.
Enmore, NSW 2042
61 (02) 95198237
www.amazingpaper.com.au
amazing_paper@bigpand.com

Birdsall Leather & Crafts
36 Chegwyn St.
Botany, NSW 2019
61 (02) 93166299
info@birdsall-leather.com.au

Primrose Paperworks Co-op
   Art & Craft Centre
Matora Ln.
Cremorne 2090
Sydney, NSW
www.primrose-park.com.au
primrosepaperworks@ihug.com.au

Ted Chapman & Co.
60 Nepean Dr.
P.O. Box 25
Mulgoa, NSW 2745

Victorian Bookbinders Guild
c/o Arthur Akhurst
17 Cheniston Rd.
Mt. Macedon, Victoria
61 (03) 54261555

Will's Quills
1/166 Victoria Ave.
Chatswood, NSW
61 (02) 94192112

CANADA

The Japanese Paper Place
887 Queen St. West
Toronto, ON M6J 1G5
(416) 703-0089
washi@japanesepaperplace.com

La Papeterie St. Armand
3700 Rue St. Patrick
Montreal, PQ H4E 1A2
(514) 931-8338

Pierre Thibaudeau
R.R.1, Grantley Rd.
Chesterville, ON K0C 1H0
(613) 448-1350

FRANCE

Relma
3 Rue des Poitevins
75006 Paris
33 (01) 43 25 40 52
relma@wanadoo.fr

Rougier et Ple
13-15 Blvd. des Filles du Calvarie
75003 Paris
33 (01) 42 72 82 90
or 33 0825 160 560
commandes@artacrea.fr

GERMANY

Drucken & Lernen
Bleicherstrasse 12
D-26122 Oldenburg
49 04 41 1 63 34
drucher-wel-lernen@t-online.de

Johannes Gerstaecker Verlag GmbH
Postfach 1165
D-53774 Eitorf
49 0 22 43 889 95
info@gerstaecker.com

PHILIPPINES

C & J Specialty Papers
   (PHILS.), Inc.
1357 A. Paz corner Apacible St.
Paco, Manila
(632) 561 3756 or
(632) 561 3791
Fax: (632) 563 6737
cjsp@pacific.net.ph
www.cnjpaper.com

Quill
Level 3, Power Plant Mall
Rockwell Center
Amapola corner Estrella St.
PI-1200 Makati City
(632) 898-1433
quill@lietz.com

SWEDEN

Bokbinderimaterial
Anders Strand
Gräsholmsvägen 12
SE-693 34 Degerfors
46 586 40 990

UNITED KINGDOM

The Fine Bindery
Bridge Approach
Mill Rd.
Wellingborough, Northants
NN8 1QN
44 01933 276689
sales@finebindery.fsnet.co.uk

J. Hewit & Sons Ltd.
Kinauld Leather Works
Currie, Edinburgh
EH14 5RS
44 (0) 131 449 2206
sales@hewit.com

USA

Bookmakers
8260 Patuxent Range Rd., Suite C
Jessup, MD 20794
(301) 604-7787
bookmakers@earthlink.net

Colophon Book Arts Supplies
3611 Ryan St. S.E.
Lacey, WA 98503
(360) 459-2940
colophon@earthlink.com

Daniel Smith Fine Artists' Materials
P.O. Box 84268
Seattle, WA 98124-5568
(206) 223-9599
(800) 426-6740
sales@danielsmith.com

Talas
568 Broadway
New York, NY 10012
(212) 219-0770
info@talasonline.com

University Products
517 Main St.
Holyoke, MA 01041
(413) 532-3372
(800) 628-1912
info@universityproducts.com

ABOUT THE AUTHORS

Peter and Donna Thomas are book artists: papermakers and letterpress printers who also illustrate, illuminate, and bind their own unique books. Their research into the history of papermaking and their exploration of alternative book structures are internationally recognized. They are founding members of the Miniature Book Society and throughout their careers have been active in the leadership of both national and international book arts and papermaking organizations. Since 1977, their books have been shown in individual and group exhibitions in the U.S. and abroad under their previous imprint, The Good Book Press, and their current imprint, Peter and Donna Thomas. Their books are found in collections around the world, including the Getty Museum, the National Gallery of Art, and UC Berkeley's Bancroft Library. They have lectured and taught workshops internationally and have published books and articles on papermaking and other aspects of the book arts. They live and work in Santa Cruz, California.

ACKNOWLEDGMENTS

We have thought about writing this book for years and want to thank our publishers for giving us the opportunity. We also want to thank Gary Young of the Greenhouse Review Press, Debbie Kogan, Marlis Killerman, and all of the students that have given us feedback in our classes.

Aloha Oe Farewell to Thee, 1998. 2¾" x 1½" (7 cm x 3.8 cm). "Aloha Oe" is most likely the world's best-known song to commemorate partings. Hawaii's Queen Liliuokaulani wrote this song late in the 1800s to a haunting tune written for the Royal Hawaiian Orchestra. Sixteen hula dancers, cut like a paper doll chain, connect together to make this beautiful accordion book. The text is written in both Hawaiian and English over watercolor paintings of Hawaiian hula dancers. This book is an edition of a one-of-a-kind shaped book made by Donna in 1998. The original watercolors and calligraphy have been stunningly reproduced, using full-color laser copy technology, on the finest Cranes 100% cotton paper. The binding is a "finger book" format, covered in Hawaiian print cloth with a hula dancer label on the cover. 16 pages. 50 copies.